REVIVAL RISING

REVIVAL RISING

Preparing for the Next Great Wave of Awakening

MARK NYSEWANDER

 Seedbed

Printed in the United States of America

Cover design by Strange Last Name
Page design by PerfecType, Nashville, Tennessee

Nysewander, Mark.

Revival rising : preparing for the next great wave of awakening / Mark Nysewander. – Frankin, Tennessee : Seedbed Publishing, ©2016.

xi, 132 pages ; 21 cm.

Includes bibliographical references (pages 125-132)
ISBN 9781628243604 (paperback : alk. paper)
ISBN 9781628243611 (Mobi)
ISBN 9781628243628 (ePub)
ISBN 9781628243635 (uPDF)

1.Revivals. 2. Religious awakening--Christianity. 3. Evangelistic work. 4. Church renewal. I. Title.

BV3790 .N97 2016   269/.2   2016951638

SEEDBED PUBLISHING
Franklin, Tennessee
Seedbed.com

To the simple believers across
the earth seeking revival.

CONTENTS

Preface: A Word of Caution | ix

1 Revival Power | 5

2 Revival Life | 15

3 Revival Culture | 23

4 Revival Experience | 33

5 Revival Glory | 41

6 Revival Love | 51

7 Revival Humility | 59

8 Revival Witness | 67

9 Revival Freedom | 77

10 Revival Hope | 87

11 Revival Worldview | 97

12 What's Ahead? | 105

Appendix 1 | 109

Appendix 2 | 117

Notes | 125

PREFACE
A WORD OF CAUTION

Some few . . . experienced the power of God
and things too deep to be described.

—From the Mukti Revival[1]

Revival Rising explores the dynamics of high-
impact revivals. The above quotation from the
Mukti Revival warns of the difficulty in under-
standing these unusual dynamics. Although it can
be challenging, we must try. Even a limited knowledge of the supernatural realities in a revival can
stir us to contend for God's next wave of power.

For that reason, you must read this book with
your heart as well as your mind. If the dynamic
described in a particular chapter inspires or even
shocks you, don't push back. Instead, allow the
Spirit to excite you toward another awakening
no matter what it looks like. These dynamics are
mined from some past revivals and Paul's letters to
the churches. If you want to know the context of
one of the historic revivals mentioned, appendix 1
has a brief description.

Stories and quotations from these older revivals
are used not because they are any better than what
God might be doing now. Rather, time has proven
their lasting fruit. A contemporary move hasn't

had enough time to pass that test. In short, historic revivals are now judged legitimate even though their dynamics may still be hard to accept.

Before you begin, here's a word of caution: God still speaks through these past waves of power. As you read you might hear a voice from history calling out, *Will you pray for the next revival until it comes?*

God's call demands a response. If you hear it, I trust your answer will be a bold, "Yes."

Each wave is a revival;
it rushes forward
with impetuous haste and with exultant joy;
it carries everything before it,
and then,
having spent its strength,
recedes,
only to be succeeded by another wave,
and yet another.
To the careless onlooker
it seems as if nothing were gained,
but behind the ebb and flow of wave
is the unconquerable power
of the tide.

—James Burns
Revivals: Their Laws and Leaders[2]

REVIVAL RISING

AWARENESS OF GOD

Revival power comes in surprising force. Duncan Campbell travels the Isle of Lewis off the coast of Scotland in 1949, where revival spreads like wildfire. In one town many reject his message that there's a Savior from sin. Because so few are attending the meeting the team prays throughout the night.

I turned to a young man in the meeting and said, "I feel led of God to ask you to pray," and that dear man rose to his feet and prayed. . . . He said, "Lord, You made a promise, are You going to fulfill it? We believe that You are a covenant-keeping God, will You be true to Your covenant? You have said that You would pour water on the thirsty and floods upon the dry ground . . . and I tell Thee now that I am thirsty, oh, I am thirsty for a manifestation of the man of Thy right hand"— and then he said this—"Lord, before I sit down, I want to tell You that Your honor is at stake."

. . . Believe it, or disbelieve it—and you can verify this if you like—the house shook like a leaf, the dishes rattled on the sideboard, an elder standing beside me said, "Mr. Campbell, an earth tremor." I said, "Yes," and I pronounced the benediction immediately and walked out to find the community alive with an awareness of God.[1]

1

REVIVAL POWER

To this end we always pray for you, that our God may make you worthy of his call, and may fulfill every good resolve and work of faith by his power. . . .

—2 THESSALONIANS 1:11–12 RSV

The Urgent Need

God's power is essential for daily life, but it can't stop there. Every generation is called to go after the most forceful display of divine power. Martyn Lloyd-Jones declares, "There is no more important subject of the Christian church at this present hour, than this very question of the need of revival . . . it is second to none."[2]

It's the most important issue to us because our culture is winding down. Any spiritual energy and order we have is quickly disintegrating. Churches aren't exempt. Movements that exploded on the scene with God's power are now fossilizing into institutions.

One pastor describes his condition as "clinging to the decaying threads of a past experience." It's true. We're all living on the diminishing energy of the previous revival. We can't go much longer. That former wave has receded.

But James Burns gives us hope, suggesting that even a receding wave "is gathering in power and volume to return, and to rush further in."[3]

Revving up human effort isn't the way to bring in the next revival. Only a determination to enter God's gathering power will bring it.

Don't give up because the wave hasn't come yet. Instead, examine if you are in the early currents of that coming surge.

Something from the Other World

Even if you're anxious because everything seems to be winding down, is revival really what you want? Often most of us simply desire a small blessing added to our human efforts. We seek God for a little boost.

But participants in past revivals describe it as anything but a little boost. David Brainerd says, "I stood amazed at the influence that seized the audience almost universally and could compare it to nothing more aptly than the irresistible force of a mighty torrent. . . ."[4]

"There is something there from the other world," explained a witness of the Welsh Revival. "You cannot say whence it came or whether it is going, but it moves and lives and reaches for you all the time."[5]

Frank Bartleman, attending the Azusa Street Revival, confesses, "I have stopped more than once within two blocks of the place and prayed for strength before I dare go on. The presence of the Lord was so real."[6]

These people don't speak of a slight blessing. This is supernatural power taking over. It's what Paul wants for the Thessalonians. His earlier letter tells how the gospel first arrives in the area. It comes "with power, and with the Holy Spirit" (1 Thess. 1:5). That's an irresistible force, not a slight bump.

Jesus promises the same. He tells his disciples, "But you will receive power when the Holy Spirit comes on you. . . ." (Acts 1:8).

Paul and Jesus agree. Revival power isn't nebulous. It's God's dynamic energy!

Read Acts. Believers constantly go after Holy-Spirit-coming-on-you power. They want outpourings that "pervade the atmosphere like a contagion, and burst out in unexpected places as if carried by unseen hands."[7]

Maybe you settle for less because all you've ever known is a small boost. This misunderstanding of power also affects our churches. We only desire a bit of help but God intends more. He wants us to know a power that's moving, living, and reaching.

Evan Roberts as a young adult encounters this very power and then sees it impact the townships of Wales. Starting in 1904, a revival tsunami advances for a year and a half. One five-week period records more than twenty thousand people come into the kingdom of God. From his experience,

Roberts declares, "revival comes from knowledge of the Holy Spirit and the way of co-working with him which enables him to work in revival power."[8]

Get specific like Evan Roberts. Start co-working with the Spirit. Begin by asking for his power. Trust the Father's promise. Who knows? What starts in you may take over an entire community.

Revival on the Shelf

Even if we are aware a revival wave is something powerful, we can still misunderstand it as being rare.

The letter to the Ephesians encourages continual infilling of the Spirit's power (see Ephesians 5:18). Paul prays more power for the Thessalonians even though months earlier they had experienced a strong move of God. He's always expecting more.

Here is God's intended pattern: grow steady in grace but also expect surges of the Spirit's power. If we're not going for more encounters, energy starts to recede.

Even churches consider revival power rare. Charles Spurgeon warns of those who think revivals shouldn't be expected every day. "That is the very reason why we do not get them," Spurgeon roars. "If we had learned to expect them we should no doubt obtain them. But we put them on the shelf, as being curiosities of scripture history. . . ."[9]

I was saved at a camp meeting that comes from the Holiness Revival. It has gathered for more than one hundred twenty-five years. There's a tendency among us who now attend to dismiss the original wave of power that started the camp as a past curiosity. Revival has become something embedded in the hard rock of history.

Whether your tradition is Holiness, Pentecostal, mainline denomination, or Charismatic, don't presume the historic revival that birthed your movement is no longer available. God still moves his people forward by waves of revival.

Repent of making it rare. Expect the Spirit to come in power for this time in history.

Undercurrents of Faith

God releases revival, but don't assume you have no part to play in it. Even though revival is supernatural you bear a responsibility in its coming.

Revival is like other expressions of God's power, only it's bigger! You're involved in healing. Jesus says to heal the sick. It, too, is supernatural, but God comes on the undercurrents of your faith. When you believe, healing is frequent. When you don't, it becomes rare.

Revival is the same. If you disengage from the process hoping God will do it alone, you misunderstand revival. You must contribute toward its coming.

Paul says you contribute by offering your resolve. That doesn't mean you simply wish things were better. Resolve is much stronger. It means you purpose to see revival.

Maybe you would like to see revival but there's no resolve. In fact, you feel a million miles away from even wanting it. Charles Finney can help. He says to take the little impulse you find and ask God why you're so weak. The Spirit might show you something like ingratitude, doubt, fear, or self-interest. Turn from what weakens you and ask for forgiveness. Then expect God to increase your resolve for a display of goodness.[10]

Start today. If you have no resolve, offer God the two things you have: repentance and faith. Watch him transform your weak impulses into a growing desire for revival. Keep asking until the Spirit forges your desire into a determined purpose.

Duncan Campbell is the pastor mentioned earlier who was "clinging to the decaying threads of a past experience." With that faint impulse he repents and believes God to increase resolve. One morning the Spirit surprisingly comes to him through the undercurrents of his faith. He explains that "wave after wave of divine consciousness came over me and the love of the Savior flooded my being."[11]

But it doesn't end there. Beginning in 1949, Duncan Campbell and countless others see a massive wave of God's goodness come on their collective resolve. The Isle of Lewis in the Hebrides is covered with revival power. Describing the effects of this wave of power, Campbell reports, "Of the hundreds who found Jesus Christ at that time, 75 percent of them were gloriously saved before they came near a meeting, before they heard a single sermon from myself or from any other minister in the parish, the power of God was moving. . . ."[12]

If you believe we need a movement of God's power in our day, do as Duncan Campbell did. Offer God your weak impulse. Trade your "decaying threads" for a purpose that won't relent until revival comes.

Lord Jesus Christ, revive me! I repent of my weak resolve and ask your forgiveness. Send on me the irresistible force of your Spirit. Empower me to pursue revival until I see it.

HOLY ATMOSPHERE

Revival life sparks the 1970 Asbury Revival. In chapel a student shares how God is awakening and cleansing his heart. Revival takes over the Kentucky campus, causing all classes to be suspended. Below are selected entries from one student's journal of the one hundred and eighty-five hours in chapel.

I sit in the middle of a contemporary Pentecost. A few moments ago there came a spontaneous movement of the Holy Spirit. . . . The scene is unbelievable. The altar has been flooding with needy souls time and time again

Two and one-half hours have passed. A joyous religion. Hands in the air. Pointed toward God— He never fails. . . .

Seven hours have passed. . . . A seminary student yearns for God to move in the seminary. There is a quiet, yet beautiful Spirit here right now. . . . People are kneeling in front of seats. . . .

Exactly twenty-six hours have passed. The altar has just been flooded with souls. Deep repentance. Unusual Spirit of holiness at this moment . . .

Forty-eight hours have passed. Almost fifteen hundred people here in Hughes. The altar is filled. . . .

Seventy-two hours have passed. Revival has spread to other Christian campuses. This revival is taking a national form. . . .

106 hours have passed . . . 11:15 p.m. 700 to 800 people in Hughes . . .

There is a very holy atmosphere here.[1]

2

REVIVAL LIFE

I pray that out of his glorious riches he may
strengthen you with power through his Spirit
in your inner being, so that Christ may dwell
in your hearts through faith.

—EPHESIANS 3:16–17

Revival Within

A catalyst exists that triggers revival. It's what
launches the Welsh Revival, the revival during
Whitfield's and Wesley's day, the Moravian Revival,
and countless others. Behind all these outpourings is a believer experiencing heart revival.
C. F. Bardley writes, "The great revivals of history
. . . have all been the result of a new personal devo-
tion to Jesus Christ, a deep, intimate, and glorious
experience."[2]

When you express the desire for a national
awakening, the Spirit is moving you to first seek
inner revival. He's looking for a life that triggers
the next wave. Norman Grubb speaks of revival as

"an everyday affair right down within the reach of everyday folks to be experienced in our hearts. . . ."[3]

If you wonder how you get revival in your heart, examine Paul's prayer. These petitions declare what must happen. But also notice how revival life is similar to a general awakening. "For that which is found common to all great movements," declares one writer, "is likely to be present in the most minute ones."[4]

What are the common characteristics of this minute revival within the heart?

I Was on Fire

Paul first prays for an inner surge of power. So start asking for the same. It is how revival life begins.

The Spirit's surge of power is common in historic revivals. Describing an outpouring at Yale College in 1796, it is said that the revival "shook the institution to its center."[5]

What happens on a campus can also take place within. God's power shakes your life at the center. If you don't know the Spirit's fullness, begin there. Ask God to fill you. If you are filled with the Spirit, believe for another surge. Revival life isn't one petition. It's a lifestyle. You're on an unrelenting quest for more.

Evan Roberts starts the quest that eventually shakes his inner world. "I felt a living force coming into my bosom," he reports. "This grew and grew and I was almost bursting. . . . From that time I was on fire with a desire to go through all Wales. . . ."[6]

The Spirit's surge of power is what advances the church. Martin Luther's reformation propels salvation by faith. A missionary movement springs from the Moravian Revival. Holiness spreads with the Wesleyan Revival. The Azusa Street Revival continues to release spiritual gifts through the nations.

That's why James Burns proclaims, "All progress we perceive is a progress through revival."[7] "All progress" not only includes church history but your life as well. Personal advances in glorifying Christ come from the Spirit's push within. Spiritual discipline is important but the Spirit's surge of power is equally essential. "At every forward step in your progress," Charles Finney writes, "you must have a fresh anointing of the Holy Spirit through faith."[8]

If your progress toward glorifying Jesus is stalled, change your lifestyle. Go after revival within. Start this quest and expect a shaking to the center.

Jesus Walked In

Paul says inner revival is about Christ dwelling in you. What does he mean? As believers Christ already dwells within.

The concern isn't whether Christ dwells in the heart but how he dwells there. Spiritual dullness comes because Jesus no longer dwells supremely in the heart. The problem is that our competing interests, sinful passions, hurts, and disappointments collect in the heart. It becomes so cluttered that any affection for Jesus is soon buried under all the stuff. These distractions overwhelm us and it becomes impossible to clean the mess up.

But revival cleanses the heart of clutter. The Spirit erupts with a supreme passion for Jesus that exalts him over everything.

In historic awakenings this happens to entire communities. The Asbury Revival brings a sense of Jesus' majesty that excites the campus. Distractions are washed away. The college president, Dennis Kinlaw, likens it to Jesus himself walking into the auditorium.

Some revivals bring intense shaking. Jonathan Edwards, in 1741, writes of the one in Northampton. He reports frequently seeing "a house full of outcries, fainting, convulsions and such like, both with distress, and also with admiration and joy."[9]

Reaction to Jesus' presence goes either way. There's the distress of separation or the joy of nearness. But here's the point. When the Spirit works in your heart with either joy or conviction, receive what is happening.

If you reject this excitement, whether it's difficult or joyous, you shut down revival life. Never dismiss the Spirit's work as emotional fluff. He is stirring you toward Jesus. Charles Finney warns, "There is so little *principle* in the Church, so little firmness and stability of purpose, that unless it is greatly excited, it will go back from the path of duty, and do nothing to promote the glory of God."[10]

Don't settle for a hoarder's heart. Seek the Spirit's surge. Let him excite you toward a love for Jesus that shakes the clutter out.

Inspired Obedience

When the Spirit stirs your heart, there's a way to secure the benefits of personal revival. Paul says to grasp the next dimension of Christ's love.

In historic awakenings people start choosing in new ways. There's a willingness to obey not seen before. Three years after the Asbury Revival, 41 percent of the student body considers full-time ministry as opposed to 25 percent before the revival. The Spirit prompts new levels of obedience.[11]

This also happens with heart revival. The Spirit doesn't excite you for the thrill of it. He's awakening you to choose God's will. When revival's blessing flows, Evan Roberts says, "Do what the Holy Spirit prompts without hesitation or fear. Obedience: prompt, implicit, unquestioning obedience at whatever cost."[12]

A friend with his family works in Asia among an isolated people group. His decision to choose this frontier of love comes in revival. An outpouring so excites his heart with Jesus' majesty he is inebriated in the Spirit for three days. Revival not only thrills his heart, it brings a willingness to go.

Obedience isn't automatic but inspired. The Spirit won't make you obey. He moves you. Refusal is still possible.

In 1996, a wave of revival moving across the world comes to my little town. The outpouring shakes the community to its core. Stirred by the revival I hear God's call to choose the Spirit's power, but I don't because of people's opinion and reaction. Though willingness is piqued I still refuse to get into the wave.

Months later, I find myself in Toronto, at the very epicenter of the revival. In kindness God whispers, "Don't stand there, get in." This time as my heart is awakened, I obey. That simple act of obedience opens countless frontiers of Christ's love.

The Spirit empowers you to choose wholly for God. John Wesley chooses to turn from his reputation as a respectable Anglican and preach in the fields. Jonathan Goforth chooses to seek a fellow missionary and apologize for wrong behavior. Lost people who previously had no interest in Jesus, run to him as Lord. Believers start choosing radical obedience.

Pray for revival life. Let the Spirit excite you with Jesus' presence. Secure what he's inspiring and choose the next frontier of Christ's love. Who knows? You may be the trigger for God's next wave of power.

Lord Jesus Christ, revive me! Release an inner surge of your Spirit. Excite my heart with your presence. Inspire me to keep seeking revival.

TIDE OF MIGHTY GRACE

Revival culture is a value of the American camp meeting from the days of Cane Ridge. One such gathering in the Holiness Revival starts at Landisville, Pennsylvania, in 1873. Midway through the encampment a group in a tent pray for a breakthrough of revival power.

Brother Thompson had suggested that the disciples of Jesus here might reach a position of dependence and humble faith in which "the promise of the Father" would be fulfilled in a most extraordinary manner. "Get down low at his feet," he continued to exhort "The power is promised; Jesus is in the midst; God the Father is willing; the Holy Ghost is waiting; it is coming—O Lord, fill us now!"

The people by scores sank to the ground. Some were utterly overpowered with "speech-less awe" and others realized the mysterious action of sacred fire on their inmost nature, purging away the dross and purifying them, even as gold is refined.

The reporter we sent in to the meeting to take notes, failed to bring us a connected or coherent narrative. His pencil and notebook fell among the straw and soon he was "laid out" himself, with the tide of mighty grace running over him.[1]

3

REVIVAL CULTURE

Are you so foolish? After beginning with the
Spirit, are you now trying to attain your goal
by human effort?

—Galatians 3:3

The Age of the Spirit

Paul cautions against abandoning a revival culture.
Unfortunately, most today don't even recognize
this culture as a possibility.

Some go so far as to justify the absence of
revival using the New Testament letters. They
argue that these writings don't expect revival
because they're not calling people into the Spirit's
power as the book of Acts shows.

But there's a reason these letters don't intro-
duce revival. The churches they address already
have it. The apostles are showing how to main-
tain a revival culture, not get it. Be careful! Our
Western prejudice against God's power can keep us
from a revival culture.

Beginning at Pentecost, Peter declares revival as the culture that advances God's purposes toward the return of Jesus. "We are still living in the age of the Spirit," declares Stephen Olford. "Pentecost was not just a day; it was the beginning of a dispensation."[2]

If we settle for less, it's a refusal of God's plan. We are called to believe together for Holy Spirit power.

Embracing Human Effort

In Galatia, the believers experience this culture because miracles manifest there (Gal. 3:5). They receive the same "promise of the Spirit" Jesus gave his disciples (Gal. 3:14). The church is encouraged to keep walking in the Spirit (Gal. 5:25).

Even with revival as their culture something's not right. Paul addresses them in Galatians 3:1 as "dear idiots of Galatia."[3] What has him upset?

It seems some believers are abandoning the Spirit. They want a culture built on human effort. Paul reminds them how revival first came. It didn't arrive by some great human accomplishment. Revival broke out because these people believed God for his power.

Like the Galatians, we, too, have a history of revival. Dig deep enough into your tradition and you'll unearth revival. Gilbert Egerton explains, "There is not a branch of the Church of Jesus Christ which deserves mention in the pages of ecclesiastical history that was not launched into existence on the tide of a great awakening."[4]

If God's power launched our movements, why do we now settle for another culture? During the Asbury Revival, Dennis Kinlaw declares, "Give me one divine moment when God acts and I say that moment is far superior to all the human efforts of man throughout the centuries."[5]

But today we're so entangled in our human efforts that divine moments aren't even considered. Paul wants to know who put this spell on us. Our condition is worse than the believers in Galatia. They know revival, but many today don't. Revival is so foreign to us it isn't even a blip on our radar.

Since we are ignorant of this reality, how can we make revival our culture? Jonathan Goforth, missionary to China, shows us. He, too, is embedded in human effort. Goforth's fruitless ministry annoys him. Frustration leads him to study scriptures about God's power. He also pours over the autobiography of Charles Finney. Revival becomes such an obsession his wife fears he will have a mental breakdown.

But Goforth's quest for God's power pays off. In 1908 it sparks an outpouring of the Spirit. Tens of thousands in the provinces of China come to Jesus. This man, once totally ignorant of revival, now promises, "The principle is clear that any group of seeking Christians may receive the full blessing of Pentecost."[6]

"Any group" means us! Like Goforth, seek this same standard. The antidote against a culture of human effort is your faith. Believe God for Holy Spirit power. Ask him to revive the culture of New Testament churches.

Humility Attracts Power

Believers at Corinth also have a local culture of revival. Planted with a demonstration of the Spirit's power, the church lacks no spiritual gift (1 Cor. 1:7). They are a dwelling of the Spirit and receive Paul's most detailed instructions on spiritual gifts (1 Cor. 2:4; 3:16; 12:14).

But there's something eating at their culture. It's human pride. The Spirit's work is being decimated by self-interest. Outside leaders are corrupting the church with their egos. Frank Bartleman warns the people at Azusa Street about this cancer. "Let us get built up by a sense of our own importance and we are gone," he cautions. "History repeats itself in this connection. God has always sought a humble people. He can use no other."[7]

The malignancy of self spreads through Corinth by eloquent speech, personal enrichment, showmanship, and personality endorsements. People even question Paul's leadership because he's doesn't demonstrate this same self-promotion.

Paul has nothing to do with it. Instead, he recalls how revival first showed up in Corinth. The power that turns everything upside down came through a weak man. Humility attracts God's power, not human importance (1 Cor. 2:1–5)!

Today churches side with the Corinthians against Paul. Promotion of reputation, strength, and wealth is openly endorsed.

Humble yourself before the God of all surpassing power! You are impotent to engineer the one culture needed. Only the Spirit makes a revival culture.

On April 15, 1906, Frank Bartleman walks into the first gathering of the Pentecostal Revival. Guess what culture he discovers? "There was a general spirit of humility manifested in the meeting," he reports. "They were taken up with God. Evidently the Lord had found his little company at last. . . ."[8]

Revival comes among nameless, faceless people offering their lives to the God of power. Repent of self-importance and enter God's "little company."

Explore the Supernatural

Believers at Thessalonica have a revival culture as well. They experience joy in the Spirit even under persecution. Since Paul's departure the region is talking of the radical transformation of this community. It's a model for all churches (1 Thess. 1:5–10).

This early picture of a church exhibits Holy Spirit power. Paul wants these believers to continue in their culture. He instructs them to never "put out the Spirit's fire" or despise prophecy. He encourages these believers to "test everything" (1 Thess. 5:19–22).

Today's overly cautious church can quickly shut down the Spirit's work. In the West a culture of caution is rampant. We quickly judge the Spirit's slightest move as dangerous and totally avoid it. Martyn Lloyd-Jones warns about this anti-supernatural arrogance. "What do we know about these great manifestations of the Holy Spirit?" he asks. "We need to be very careful lest we be found to be fighting against God, lest we be guilty of quenching the Holy Spirit of God."[9]

Don't misinterpret Paul's advice to "test every-thing." It's not permission to reject revival. You're not being deputized to pat down the Holy Spirit if he shows up. One translation says "explore every-thing." That makes better sense. You take a car on a test drive not because you fear it. Rather, you like it and want to see what the car can do. When the Spirit comes in power, test what he can do![10]

Exploring God's power is revival culture. You can't limit God to what you know. Your knowl-edge doesn't exhaust God's display of power. Leave caution behind and cross into expectancy.

John Wesley records the moment revival breaks out in 1739. He doesn't fear the Spirit's power but test drives it. Finishing a sermon, he says, "I called upon God to confirm His word. Immediately, to my surprise, someone nearby cried out with utmost vehemence, as though in agony of death." After prayer, the man who is overcome by God experi-ences unspeakable joy.

A week later after preaching, he invites the people to explore revival power with him. "I asked them to pray that if this was the will of God, He would bear witness to His word. Immediately one, then another, and another sank to the earth. They dropped on every side as if thunderstruck."

That evening God's power continues to accel-erate. Wesley tells, "Almost before we called upon God to set to His Seal, He answered." Another man is overpowered by the Spirit.[11]

Wesley explores revival for nearly fifty years. He transfers this culture across the ocean, where God's power explodes through the Methodist camp meetings. It is boldness that plants revival cultures throughout the new nation and brings wave after wave of revival.

Lord Jesus Christ, revive me! Overcome all my dependence on human effort, self-promotion, and fearful caution. Keep filling me with your Spirit. Embolden me to explore supernatural breakthroughs. Raise up a people who, together, pray for revival.

AN INVISIBLE HAND

Revival experience comes to Charlotte Chapel in Edinburgh, Scotland. After visiting the Welsh Revival, Joseph Kemp encourages his church to start praying for a local outpouring. In January of 1907, it culminates with an encounter of God's presence in an ongoing prayer meeting.

To the curious, the meetings appear disorderly; but to those who are in them and of them, there is order in the midst of disorder. The confusion never gets confused; the meetings are held by an invisible Hand. . . .

While the work has been chiefly confined to the saints of God, there have been numerous conversions. But these have all taken place during the time of prayer, and prayer usually of a tumultuous sort. One does not readily take in the meaning of simultaneous praying, in a meeting of from 100 to 200 people, full to overflowing of a strong desire to pour out their hearts before the Lord. . . .

We appeal for a freedom of the Holy Spirit on our gatherings, and, as one eminent writer had said, "God save us, lest we civilize the Holy Spirit out of our churches."

This awakening and quickening was so spontaneous and almost unlooked for that we are compelled to acknowledge its divine origin. It has not passed off and vanished in mere sentiment; nor like a wave of emotion proved itself transient and unreal. It abides.[1]

4

REVIVAL EXPERIENCE

> . . . and to know this love that surpasses
> knowledge . . .
>
> —Ephesians 3:19

Promoting Disorder

The petition above is very odd. How can you know
what can't be known?

Paul here speaks of an experiential knowledge that surpasses rational thought. This type of
knowledge forcefully rushes forward in the wave
of revival.

It also attracts revival's strongest criticism. The
General Association of the Colony of Connecticut
takes a vote in June 1745. The decision advises
pastors not to welcome George Whitfield because
he promotes disorder.[2]

The General Association is rejecting the
churning, vibrant experiences of revival. Back in
England, John Wesley is labeled an enthusiast
because of these experiences. The criticisms aren't

just about doctrine but the experience people have when the doctrine is preached.

Such objections continue today. Churches are comfortable with rational knowledge but very nervous about experiential knowledge. Though the caution is now more subtle than in Whitfield's day, it's just as effective. Constant warnings get the same results as an official condemnation. It creates pushback from revival experience.

This prejudice puts us on the wrong side of history. Imagine being transported back to a revered awakening. You actually witness the experiences under a revivalist like Edwards, Whitfield, or Wesley.

Suppose you're watching William Carvosso in the British Great Awakening when he's sanctified by the Spirit. Carvosso stuns you as he exclaims, "a heavenly influence filled the room . . . refining fire went 'through my heart' . . . I was emptied of self and sin and filled with God." He then shouts out, "This is what I wanted. I have now got a new heart."[3]

Will you write off this dramatic scene under John Wesley's leadership as disorder?

It Was Unspeakable

We often hesitate about revival experience, fearing it carries with it a flood of fanaticism. That certainly happens at times but it doesn't mean all revivals are displays of self-absorption. Henry Fish says the destructive flood caused by rain doesn't mean all rain should be rejected. "On the whole," he says, defending rain, "the atmospheric arrangement is a good one."[4]

The "atmospheric arrangement" of revival is also good, but constant warnings about selfishness cause us to avoid it. Moves of the Spirit transforming thousands get dismissed as the sickness of our "me" culture.

Jonathan Edwards defends revival experience even when it involves physical manifestations. To him such experiences aren't selfishness but encounters with Jesus. He says that, "a true sense of the glorious Excellency of the Lord Jesus Christ, and of his wonderful dying love, and the exercise of a truly spiritual love and joy, should be such as very much to overcome the bodily strength."[5]

Sociologist Margaret Poloma interviews people during the Toronto Blessing. Many participants had such a strong encounter they fell to the floor. In her findings 92 percent report greater love for Jesus because of their revival experience.[6]

There's a classic book from the Holiness Revival entitled *Perfect Love*. In the work, J. A. Wood describes the Spirit's power to free us from self-interest. As I read it, to me the content seems somewhat dry. I wonder how this academic doctrine ignites one of history's most dynamic revivals.

Turning to the final chapter, everything suddenly makes sense to me. There Wood tells of a personal experience that thrusts him into the Holiness Revival. The dynamic isn't in a doctrine but an experience. Doctrine simply defines what God is doing and shows how to enter the experience.

Here is Wood's own attempt to describe an experience that surpasses knowledge: "I was conscious that Jesus had me in his arms," he says, "and that the Heaven of heavens was streaming through and through my soul in such beams of light and overwhelming love and glory, as can never be uttered." As this wave starts crashing over others, Wood reports that "every half hour during that whole night the glorious power of God came down from the upper ocean in streams as sweet as heaven. At times it was unspeakable and almost unendurable."[7]

This is the encounter that delivers Wood from self-interest. Even though it's turbulent, how can the experience possibly be selfish?

Expect God to bring encounters surpassing what you already know.

A Felt Encounter

Experience is also dismissed as emotionalism. Since emotions are often judged faulty, we're warned not to trust revival experiences.

In 1996 I'm ministering with a team of college students at a camp meeting. Late in the night a student awakens me and reports the Holy Spirit is coming on young people in the dorm. The powerful experiences free the youth from their dull secular lives with God's unspeakable joy.

The next evening an evangelist warns of emotionalism in the camp. He doesn't demand the young people stop encountering God. But his caution pours doubt on the experiential knowledge they enjoy.

John Wesley does the opposite. He wants people to know an experience that reaches their emotions.

Responding to charges of emotionalism, Wesley declares, "The very thing which Mr. Shinstra calls fanaticism, is no other than heart-felt religion; in other words, 'righteousness, and peace, and joy in the Holy Ghost.' These must be felt, or they have no being."[8]

Revival experience goes deep. At our core God secures his purpose. Yet prejudice against excitement keeps many from Holy Spirit encounter. You can't enjoy God's experiential kiss if you constantly push away from emotions.

In Wesley's later years a revival comes to Everton, England. Wesley tells of a woman "so overwhelmed with the love of God, that she sunk down and appeared as one in a pleasant sleep . . . she frequently laughed while she saw his glory." Then he writes, "I no sooner sat down by her than the Spirit of God poured the same blessedness into my soul."[9] He never grows tired of getting in the wave.

Avoid revival experience as emotionalism and you reject divine encounter. Instead of watching from a distance, do as Wesley. Come near the fires of the Spirit. Who knows? God might pour the same blessedness into your soul.

Experience Is Irrational

Some believe all revival experience should be denied. They don't mean deny you had an experience but deny it holds any value. Since experience ranks far below the rational, you should judge it as shallow and irrational.

Paul doesn't show this bias. He prays his churches experience Christ's love. He's not the only one. The Orthodox tradition sees theology as more than rational doctrine. Theology comes from a participation in the realities of God's presence. In other words, experiential knowledge undergirds theological thought.[10]

Where do we get this Western prejudice against revival experience? Martyn Lloyd-Jones thinks Thomas Aquinas of the twelfth century is one influence. Aquinas's theological work, *Summa Theologica*, is foundational for Western church thinking. It teaches that God can't be known directly through experience but only indirectly by five outside proofs.

Aquinas spends his adult life demonstrating how God is only known through rational thought. Then one day he experiences God! After his encounter Aquinas stops writing. A friend asked him why he doesn't finish the remaining volumes of his theology. "I can do no more" he responds. "Such things have been revealed to me that all I have written seems as straw and I now await the end of my life."[11]

One encounter surpasses all the knowledge found in his volumes of theology. Aquinas is ruined by God's presence. This is the knowledge we're made to experience.

Lord Jesus Christ, revive me! Forgive me for pushing you away. Encounter me, Lord! Encounter me fully with your perfect love. Send a wave of revival surpassing what we already know.

HIS MAJESTY AND HIS LOVE

Revival glory settles over the community of Bradford, England, in the late 1800s. Elijah Cadman, a commissioner in the Salvation Army, reports on a particular phenomenon accompanying God's manifest presence.

There were never, in my experience of the "Glory Fits" any warning signs. A meeting might be "hard" . . . and then, in an instant the power of God would descend on us, sinners be hushed into awe and be overcome by the sense of His majesty and His love. . . .

I have led meetings where the Holy Spirit was manifest in such power that half the soldiers present were in "Glory Fits" and I had to cling, nearly helpless, to the platform rail, lifting my heart and crying inwardly all the time to God to shepherd my people. Conversions always took place in such meetings. . . .

I was sure it was a manifestation of God. If they'd cursed or sworn in or coming out of the "Fit" or after the cures, or their action and lives had been bad, I should have known 'twas the Devil at work and gone after him tooth and nail. But these people fell down praising God and giving Him glory and when they came to their bodily senses they did the same, all their words and actions showing humility before Him and love to Him and His Son, and afterwards there was a great tenderness and gentleness shown towards their neighbors and their enemies.[1]

5

REVIVAL GLORY

And if what was fading away came with glory, how much greater is the glory of that which lasts! Therefore, since we have such a hope, we are very bold.

—2 Corinthians 3:11–12

Overcome by God's Presence

Glory is the forceful manifestation of God's presence.[2] There's a glory available to us far more forceful than what Moses encounters at Mount Sinai. It comes in revival.

Describing the effects of revival on the Isle of Lewis, Duncan Campbell says, "I have known men out in the fields, so overcome by the sense of God that they were found prostrate on the ground."[3]

Paul encourages a bold pursuit of the greater glory (2 Cor. 3:13), but, like Moses, many of us veil it instead. We cover up God's manifest presence with our hesitation. This caution takes over because glory has a cost. In fact, it's so costly many avoid it altogether. See if any reluctance resides within you. If so, admit it and ask God for a new determination to pay the price of glory.

A Vacation from Heaven

Mother Riggs, with others, encounters the revival glory of Azusa Street. A friend reports, "She was convinced that the glory they experienced was a part of heaven and she was walking in it, living it and breathing it."[4] Mother Riggs is right. In revival we taste heaven on earth because heaven fully displays God's presence.

A person from the Welsh Revival agrees. "It is glorious," he exclaims. "I can imagine if John Wesley and Howell Harris wanted a holiday outside of heaven they would spend it in south Wales."[5]

Revival glory is a sample of the coming age, when heaven is joined to earth. If this is true, why the hesitation? One reason is that unusual manifestations often accompany revivals. Let's be clear. These phenomena are not God's presence. They're simply reactions in the physical realm triggered by revival glory.

At times there can be strong sensations like warmth, laughter, or heaviness. Dreams, visions, or even angelic encounters may happen. Physical manifestations such as falling out, shaking, drunkenness, or weeping are expressed. On some occasions there are even visible signs like fire, cloud, or an earth tremor.

Although a manifestation indicates God's presence has forcefully come, its unusual nature causes alarm. That's why Moses veils his face. The Hebrew people witness awesome phenomena like smoke, fire, and earth tremors surrounding God's glory at Mount Sinai. A severe warning is given not to go near the mountain (Exod. 19:16–23). All this spooks the people. So much so, they won't even talk to Moses because of the strange glow of glory on his face. Moses accommodates their fear and veils the glory.

I have my own witness of a move of the Spirit where children start dreaming and having visions of Jesus' return. The adults panic. These experiences create concern and immediately the meeting is shut down. One lady explains that kids should only be introduced to the Spirit but not go too deep.

Banning all unusual and unexpected signs guarantees a rejection of God's forceful presence. Revival glory isn't always comfortable. "If we find a revival that is not spoken against," declares Charles Finney, "we had better look again to ensure that it is a revival."[6]

To be jolted from our stupor this country may require another shocking wave of revival like Cane Ridge. One eyewitness there reports seeing eight hundred people "struck down" and lying under God's power from fifteen minutes to six, eight, or ten hours.[7]

Whether the next revival comes with such force or not, we can't afford to veil it with reluctance. God alone knows what it will take to awaken our nation. Accept divine wisdom no matter where it leads.

Off-Centered

Moses encounters glory in the tent of meeting (Exod. 34:30–35). No tent of meeting now exists for us, but there is a better place. We have the Holy Spirit! If we enter totally into the Spirit's fullness it means increasing glory (2 Cor. 3:16). Look behind any revival. There you find a believer or a group entering the Spirit's fullness.

Charles Finney carries revival glory all over the northeastern United States. It's ignited by his experience in the Spirit. He writes that "the Holy Spirit descended upon me in a manner that seemed to go through me, body and soul. I could feel the impression, like a wave of electricity, going through and through me. . . . It seemed like the very breath of God."[8]

If entering into fullness results in this kind of glory, why do we hesitate? Paul says that where the Spirit is there's freedom (2 Cor. 3:17). In other words, the Spirit comes in fullness because we give him freedom to move as he desires. For many that's a problem

It's a problem because the Spirit's freedom has a price. Those around won't always understand us. The liberating ways of God's Spirit can cost us acceptance and at times our reputation. The Spirit's freedom in Charles Finney leads to an effigy of him being burned. "You will be called eccentric and probably you will deserve it," Finney warns us. "Probably you will really be eccentric. I never knew a person who was filled with the Spirit that was not called eccentric. . . . They act under different influences, take different views, are moved by different motives, led by a different spirit."[9]

"Eccentric" means off center. Your center is no longer the values of this age or even the nice values of Western Christianity. You give the Spirit freedom to move your life toward God's glory.

Our tent of meeting is the Spirit's fullness. Entering in has a cost. The Spirit's freedom in you may be misunderstood but it's worth the risk.

Strong Men Die Hard

God's glory exalts his Son. That's exactly what happens to Moses under the tent of meeting. In the glory he sees and worships the Son as God. Check it out. One verse of Exodus declares Moses can't see God and live (Exod. 33:20). But another reports Moses sees the Lord because he speaks to him face-to-face (Exod. 33:11). Which is it?

It's both. The Father who is the unseen expression of God, reveals the Son who is the visible expression of God. It's the Son who Moses sees face-to-face and calls Lord. The visible expression of the Son also appears to Abraham, Jacob, and many others, and they all call him Lord as well. This Son eventually comes in the body of Jesus from Nazareth and now we call him our Lord and God.

Jonathan Edwards says the Father sends revival glory to draw our attention to his now resurrected and ascended Son. "When God manifests himself with such glorious power, in a work of this nature," Edwards explains, "he appears especially determined to put honor upon his Son and to fulfill his oath that he has sworn to him, that he would make every knee to bow . . . to him."[10]

So if God's glory exalts Jesus Christ as Lord, why are we reluctant about revival? It's because revival comes with a cost. Revival glory not only reveals the Son but changes us into his likeness (2 Cor. 3:18). If we want to keep our selfish ways, we'll avoid this transforming power of glory.

Frank Bartleman of the Azusa Street Revival describes the work of glory going on there. "Even very good men came to abhor themselves in the clearer light of God," he reports. "They had so much to die to. So much reputation and good works. But when God got through with them they gladly turned a new page and chapter. That was the reason they fought so hard. Death is not at all a pleasant experience. And strong men die hard."[11]

God's glory in the face of Jesus shatters your old ways. Revival is not just exciting, it's devastating. But the devastation is glorious. It breaks open fresh experiences of new creation life. James Burns describes how a wave of revival glory overwhelms us. He says, "vast energies, hitherto slumbering, are awakened, and new forces—for long preparing under the surface—burst into being. Its tide rolls in from an unseen continent, and moves with a gathering momentum which nothing can resist."[12]

Don't fight the wave of God's glory. Surrender to it. Leave behind selfish patterns now. Expect energies of new life to "burst into being."

Bramwell Booth tells of bold believers in the early days of the Salvation Army. They risk all for an expression of revival glory. He says of them, "Thank God for the daredevils! They led us on the forward march."[13]

Today God searches for some more daredevils to move history toward the next revival.

Lord Jesus Christ, revive me! I surrender my fears, reputation, and pride. Embolden me to keep going after revival. Give a display of revival glory that becomes another Great Awakening.

EXTRAORDINARY EFFECTS

Revival love pours out on Jonathan Edwards' church in 1742. This revival under the ministry of Mr. Buell exceeds the one eight years before. A visit by George Whitfield some months earlier triggers events leading to the revival.

In the month of May, 1741, a sermon was preached to a company, at a private house. Near the conclusion of the discourse, one or two persons that were professors, were so greatly affected with a sense of the greatness and glory of divine thing they were not able to conceal it—the affections of their minds overcoming their strength, and having visible effect upon their bodies. . . .

About the beginning of February, 1742, Mr. Buell came to this town. . . . There were very extraordinary effects of Mr. Buell's labors; the people were exceedingly moved, crying out in great numbers in the meeting-house, and a great part of the congregation commonly staying in the house of God for hours after the public service. . . .

Mr. Buell continued here a fortnight or three weeks after I returned: there being still great appearances attending his labors; many in their religious affections being raised far beyond what they had ever been before: and there were some instances of persons lying in a sort of trance, remaining perhaps for a whole twenty-four hours motionless. . . .[1]

6

REVIVAL LOVE

And hope does not disappoint us, because
God has poured out his love into our hearts
by the Holy Spirit, whom he has given us.

—Romans 5:5

Revival Headaches

God expresses a love toward us and we feel it in
our hearts. Revival brings another expression of
God's love. Although this love is not directed at us,
it, too, can be felt within. This unique expression
of God's love identifies true revival. Maybe you
think it's easy to discern what's of God in revival
because of all you've read of past revivals. But past
revivals don't always give discernment.

"Revivals in the history books or in Africa
sound wonderful!" Geoff Waugh explains.
"Revivals in your backyard can be a headache!"[2]
We tend to filter out all the confusion swirling
around past and distant revivals. These sanitized
versions don't prepare us to discern what's truly of
God in a present outpouring.

A move of God is not easy to navigate. It has many twists and turns. At times it attracts lesser elements. Fortunately, God provides a north star to sail those unknown seas. Revival love is that reference point.

A Fiery Stream of Love

Jonathan Edwards tells what this expression of God's love is that shines above all else. "God hath had it much on his heart, from all eternity, to glorify his dear and only begotten son," says Edwards, "and there are some special seasons that he appoints to that end, wherein he comes with omnipotent power. . . ."[3]

Revival isn't only about God's love for you. It's about the white-water rapids of God's love toward his Son. Jesus actually prays you experience these currents of the Father's passion for him (see John 17:26).

This overpowering affection of God surging through us toward the Son is almost unbearable at times. John Wesley calls it perfect love. It's perfect because you're actually experiencing the Father's felt love for his Son. Wesley declares this unique expression of love is available to all believers. Indeed, encountering it is essential.

Perfect love fuels the revival of the late 1700s in England and the Holiness Revival in the next century. The Father's affection for his Son carries people into a sanctified expression of life that exalts Jesus.

Wesley calls believers to secure the benefit of perfect love. God's fiery passion actually softens and reshapes the human will. Many coming out of this encounter find an ability to consistently choose for Jesus.

Methodism's first American bishop, Francis Asbury, spreading holiness across America, shares his own experience, "My heart is melted into holy love, and altogether devoted to my Lord."[4]

"I sunk down motionless," reports Hester Ann Rogers, an English Methodist, "being unable to sustain the *weight* of his glorious presence and *fullness of love*."[5]

William Hunter, one of Wesley's preachers, tells of his own experience: "my love to Christ was like fire and I had such views of him as my life, my portion, my all, as swallowed me up."[6]

Daniel Steele of the Holiness Revival says, "My physical sensations . . . were like those of electric sparks passing through my bosom with slight but painless shocks, melting my hard heart into a fiery stream of love."[7]

The Father wants you to enter his love for the Son. Ask for perfect love. You already know God's great love for you in Christ. Now, expect God's fiery love for Christ in you!

Glorious Distraction

When Paul speaks of God's love being poured out, it's a dramatic picture. Martyn Lloyd-Jones explains that poured out is "a very strong term and it is the one that the apostle under divine inspiration was led to use and we must not minimize these terms."[8] The picture shows God emptying on us the full force of his love all at once. The same term is used for the Spirit's turbulent coming on the day of Pentecost. Revival love is disruptive.

Jonathan Edwards is away when revival comes a second time to Northampton. At home, his wife weeps for days because God is drawing near. On the fifth day, revival love is suddenly poured out and Sarah Edwards goes down under the massive volume of God's affection.

Four days later she wakes up in her bedroom recovering from the disruptive encounter. As friends tell her what's happening in the revival, she springs from her chair in joy and again falls under the Spirit's power. Through the night Sarah enjoys indescribable currents of God's love.

On day ten, hearing more revival news, she starts jumping for joy. God's love is so overwhelming, Sarah collapses. A while later her friends help her get around because she's so weak.

Two weeks into the revival, Sarah hears about the outpouring her husband is seeing in his ministry. God's love again overpowers her. Friends worship in her bedroom while Sarah walks around in some transported state. The next day folks share revival experiences with her and Sarah dances with delight.

Sarah tells of one of these encounters with perfect love in the night. "My heart and soul flowed out in love to Christ," she explains, "so that there seemed to be a constant flowing and reflowing of heavenly and divine love from Christ's heart to mine and I appeared to myself to float or swim in the bright, sweet beams of the love of Christ. . . . It seemed to be all that my feeble frame could withstand."[9]

The intensity of Sarah Edwards's experience isn't the point of this narrative. God's disruptive love is. If her story is offensive, it shows how little we understand the immensity of God's love for his Son.

One day every knee will bow to Jesus. Why does it surprise us if revival love buckles a few knees and reconfigures the human will? Whatever its intensity, this kind of encounter is needed.

Jonathan Edwards, America's greatest theologian, agrees. He makes sure any critic of Sarah's experience understands one thing. If they think his wife is mentally disturbed then he wants this happy mental disorder to be his forever![10]

Giving Away What God Gives

Revival love also transfers to other lives. In 1995 a visitor to the revival in Toronto reports, "God has poured His Spirit out on a people in an improbable little church, and they are now spending their time from morning to night giving away as fast as they can what God is giving to them."[11]

No ministry compares to the one flowing out of revival love. The two periods when I've seen the greatest anointing to bless others come from times of revival. The transference of love in the day of his power is second to none.

A Vero Beach radio station broadcasts an interview with Randy Clarke about the revival in Toronto.

God's power suddenly falls on those in the studio. Later the manager of the station reports, "We have received at least a dozen verified, credible, reliable comments from people who told us that when they switched on the radio, they were suddenly, unexpectedly overwhelmed by the presence of God. . . ."[12] Some of these people pull their cars off the road because the experience is so disruptive.

Does that mean God's love is only transferred in times of revival? No, but it does mean the most intense transfer comes during revival.

Therese of Lisieux experiences revival love. She says of her personal encounter, "I was seized with such a violent love for God that I cannot explain it except by saying that it was as if I had been totally plunged into fire. Oh! What fire and what sweetness at one and the same time! I was burning with love. . . ."[13]

Sometime later God shows her the calling on her life. She says, "Then, in the excess of my delirious joy, I cried out: 'O Jesus, my Love . . . at last I have found my vocation. . . . MY VOCATION IS LOVE.'"[14]

Like Therese, you're called to transfer God's love. Do it every day but also expect the day of God's power. The Spirit's turbulent flow will then disrupt nations with revival love.

Lord Jesus Christ, revive me! By the Spirit pour out on me the Father's love for you. Melt my heart "into a fiery stream of love." Empower me to believe for countless people coming to Jesus.

A FOREST OF FALLEN TREES

Revival humility manifests in 1906 during the outpouring at Azusa Street. Frank Bartleman is a Holiness preacher who witnesses those early days under William Seymour's leadership. He writes about what happens at the inception of the Pentecostal movement.

Brother Seymour generally sat behind two empty shoe boxes, one on top of the other. He usually kept his head inside the top one during the meeting, in prayer. There was no pride there. The services ran almost continuously. Seeking souls could be found under the power almost any hour, night and day. . . . The place was never closed or empty. The people came to meet God. He was always there. Hence a continuous meeting. The meeting did not depend on the human leader. . . .

God himself would give the altar call. Men would fall all over the house, like the slain in battle, or rush for the altar en masse, to seek God. The scene often resembled a forest of fallen trees. Such a scene cannot be imitated. . . . It seemed a fearful thing to hinder or grieve the Spirit. The whole place was steeped in prayer. God was in His holy temple. It was for man to keep silent. The Shekinah glory rested there. In fact, some claim to have seen the glory by night over the building.[1]

7

REVIVAL HUMILITY

But we have this treasure in jars of clay to show that this all-surpassing power is from God and not from us.

—2 CORINTHIANS 4:7

Abandoned, Dilapidated, and Damaged

God's power surpasses all others and its most forceful expression is revival. There's no power like it this side of Jesus' return.

Someone asks a visitor to the Welsh Revival what he thinks of it. "Sir, the question is not what I think of it," he answers, "but what it thinks of me, of you, and all the rest of us. For it is a real thing, this revival, a live thing which seems to have a power and a grip. . . ."[2]

This massive display of power often shows up in the same kind of place. It manifests in simple settings. The twentieth century's most extravagant outpouring is hosted in an abandoned Methodist church used as a horse stable and warehouse on a street named Azusa. In the beginning of the nineteenth century the primitive woods of Kentucky welcome God's power. The eighteenth century provides a damaged cannon factory for this power to gush toward the open fields of England. Go all the way back to the sixteenth century, and a dilapidated chapel in Wittenberg contains the thunderstorm of God's word and power.

The reason revival comes to humble places is because they house humble people. Humility is the best conductor for God's power. To be an instrument of revival, seek the posture that conveys such power. Here's how to enter revival humility.

Asking the God of Power

The most prevalent barrier to revival's coming is not bad theology. Nor does fear and ignorance pose the largest threat. You and I are the main impediments to the next wave. While desiring God's power our pride actually keeps it from coming. This pride exhibits itself in a hyper-dependence on human abilities. It distracts us from God and what he alone can do.

Addiction to human effort is deceptive because activity can bring some change. What it brings though isn't enough. Radical transformation is needed today and that will only come by another wave of God's power.

Turn from any illusion that your activities will win the day. Even if you develop excellent and professional abilities, they still won't do. Paul says you are an earthen vessel. Your purpose is to display God's power, not the latest leadership techniques.

C. G. Bevington declares, "God will not hitch his power onto the bungling, weighty, clumsy machinery of man's methods and wisdom. It's prayer that tops the reservoir of power."[3] Repent of the popular fascination with the "clumsy machinery" of human effort. Humble yourself and pray for revival. Ask God to begin with your heart.

Marie Monsen, a missionary in China, hears of revival in Korea. She asks God to send her there so she can bring it back to China. God tells her prayer, not a trip to Korea, will bring the power she wants. Monsen humbles herself and commits to pray.

The day she begins praying a force suddenly tightens around her like a boa constrictor. She cries out to Jesus and it leaves. The demonic attack convinces Monsen that prayer for revival is the highest priority. Over the next twenty years she humbly seeks God for his all-surpassing power until it comes in 1927.[4]

You may not have a demon trying to stop you from seeking revival but there's something else just as dangerous. A love affair with human effort can also strangle your cry for revival.

While G. Campbell Morgan is visiting the Welsh Revival, God admonishes him, "See what I can do without the things you are depending on, see what I can do in answer to a praying people; see what I can do through the simplest, who are ready to fall in line and depend wholly and absolutely on me."[5]

Depend on God more than your effort. Prayer is one expression of revival humility.

Drops of Power

Even when God's power comes and starts spreading, it often gets shut down. Religious or secular opposition isn't the most common threat to its survival. Again, we believers are the ones who cause revivals to cease. While we ask God for more, our pride can actually demolish what he's trying to build up. This pride manifests in a presumption that God's power is meant only for us.

Understand this. An element of revival is about us. The Spirit comes to revive and excite, so it's important we receive the fullness of his work. But the attitude that God's power is all about us will eventually stop a revival. Humility doesn't make revival all about self. It lives to transfer the all-surpassing power to others.

Paul says you are an earthen vessel carrying God's power, but the vessel doesn't have a lid to hold the power. It has a spout to give it away. The transforming power of God is also the transferable power of God. So pour it on others.

Don't wait for the full force of revival before you start. Humbly transfer what little power you now have.

After Marie Monsen is filled with the Holy Spirit, she reads in her Chinese Bible that rivers of living water will flow out of her. She knows she's filled but sees neither a river nor a trickle of power.

The Spirit brings her mind to the mighty Yangtze River. He shows how the river begins. It all starts with a tiny drop of water high in the mountains. From that revelation she begins her ministry the same way. Monsen seeks one tiny drop of power.

It comes in a time when she's helping a lady in need. Over time she sees more and more power. Monsen presses into it one person at a time. Soon she sees many drops affecting entire groups. Finally these drops merge into an overwhelming flood of revival power. "Not until later did I realize that these first cases were born with hard labor," she explains, "and that as time went on it grew easier, till at last it was almost dynamic. . . . It seemed as though the degree of spiritual power in the atmosphere was one of the reasons for the difference."[6]

Humbly transfer God's power to others even if it's one drop at a time. Do it with an expectation that someday you'll see a turbulent revival flowing through the atmosphere.

A Tremendous Overhauling

As revival comes and flows its full potential can still be aborted. Sin in leadership or heresy isn't the most significant threat to God's power.

These things are certainly serious, but the most prevalent danger is the likes of you and me. While ministering God's power, our pride can rob revival of its ultimate purpose. Pride claims all-surpassing power for itself to do with as it pleases.

Let's be frank. Western materialists are easily tempted to use anything for self-promotion and enrichment. Theologies are legitimized to endorse selfish gain. This kind of pride can quickly take over a revival with self-interest.

Paul thunders against this behavior. declaring that all-surpassing power belongs to God alone! So what should be done? Receive the power that flows through you but remember God determines its purpose. Revival humility submits to God's will even if it wrecks all selfish ambition.

A witness to Azusa Street says, "In that old building with its low rafters and bare floors, God took strong men and women to pieces and put them together again for his glory. It was a tremendous overhauling process. Pride and self assertion, self importance and self esteem could not survive there."[7]

Remember: the best conductor of all-surpassing power is a humble one. If God calls you to costly, difficult, or unknown actions, obey him. Your surrendered life can bring the next revival to fullness.

"The thing that impressed me most was the humility of the people," says another person at Azusa, "and I went to my room and got down on my knees and asked God to give me humility."[8]

Lord Jesus Christ, revive me! Give me humility. Give us a revival free of self-assertion, self-enrichment, and self-promotion. Move us all by your Spirit to choose your ways before and during revival.

REMARKABLE SEVEN WEEKS

Revival witness comes through the ministry of C. G. Bevington, a Holiness preacher of the early 1900s. In one local outpouring he does nothing but pray in a house for the members of a church. The Spirit comes to the house and gives his witness to the people.

Thus began one of the most remarkable seven weeks of my life, right there in that man's house. I never took off my clothes and never preached a sermon. I just lay day and night on my face, praying, weeping, groaning, pleading, imploring, beseeching, and besieging the throne in behalf of that M. E. membership of three hundred people. Some would get through and strike out for their relatives and friends. They would stay until the whole load got saved and sanctified. Then they would strike out after someone else.

That kept up for seven weeks—day and night. No one ate but one meal every twenty-four hours, yet someone was out in the kitchen cooking all the time. I got such a burden that I could not get up, but just lay there wherever I was praying. They would come in at times and feed me like they would a baby.

Well, they claimed there were over four hundred down there and most of them prayed through. Of all the times I ever saw, this beat anything. Some were praying, others crying, others testifying, others preaching, others shouting, others making restitution. I just lay on my face bathed in tears.[1]

8

REVIVAL WITNESS

. . . because our gospel came to you not simply with words, but also with power, with the Holy Spirit and with deep conviction.

—1 Thessalonians 1:5

Double-Barrel Testimony

Our words about Jesus Christ are most effective when coupled with another testimony. What we share needs the Spirit's witness added to ours.

Look at the first disciples. Their witness is far greater than ours. They, like us, can testify to forgiveness of sins but, unlike us, they are eyewitnesses to the ministry, crucifixion, and resurrection of Jesus (Luke 24:46–48).

Talk about a testimony. It's off the charts! Who of us has seen Jesus in his resurrected body? But with the first disciples' amazing witness, they still don't have what's needed (Luke 24:49). Jesus tells these followers with a superior witness to wait in

Jerusalem for something more. The Spirit's witness is the more.

What's true for those disciples is certainly true for us. Our personal witness is important but not enough. The Spirit's testimony must be added. Radical transformation comes through a double-barrel witness.

In the raging fires after Pentecost, Peter proclaims, "We are witnesses to these things, and so is the Holy Spirit. . . ." (Acts 5:32). He's describing revival witness.

Ask God to increase the Spirit's power until you, too, have the other witness.

A Thrilling Joy

The Spirit's witness is a tangible manifestation that shows up in two different places. Paul says the Spirit gives an inner witness. He witnesses to us the fact that we are God's children. This isn't you calling God your Father through prayer and worship. It's the Spirit manifesting a tangible evidence of your new-creation nature in Christ (see Romans 8:16–17).

Samuel Chadwick tells of the Spirit's witness within him. "There came into my soul," he writes, "a deep peace, a thrilling joy, and a new sense of power. My mind was quickened."[2] Every believer should have this internal witness. If you don't, invite the Holy Spirit to give you a tangible expression of God's nature. It will ignite your personal testimony with an inner fire.

Another place the Spirit testifies is outwardly in a public gathering. This is what happens at Pentecost. The witness is so tangible even the unbelieving bystanders sense it. Peter explains the Spirit is publicly expressing Jesus as Lord.

Days before the Moravian Revival of 1727 this kind of outward witness comes while the pastor speaks. "On Sunday, August 10, about noon, while pastor Rothe was holding the meeting at Herrnhut, he felt himself overwhelmed by a wonderful and irresistible power of the Lord, and sunk down into the dust before God, and with him sunk down the whole assembled congregation, in an ecstasy of feeling."[3]

Notice how all the people in public feel the witness at the same time. Expect an increased expression of the Spirit's testimony both inwardly and outwardly. His witness amplifies our words about Jesus.

Visible Flames of Fire

The personal and public witness of the Spirit comes to us in a variety of ways. There's his witness through our behavior. It's called the fruit of the Spirit. This fruit is not some behavior change developed by a process of spiritual discipline. It's the Spirit giving a sudden and specific manifestation of new-creation life.

Explaining the Spirit's witness, John Wesley says, "The immediate result of this testimony is, 'the fruit of the Spirit;' namely, 'love, joy, peace, longsuffering, gentleness, goodness,' and without these, the testimony itself can not continue."[4] The Spirit manifests through your behavior the character qualities of Christ. Love is the sum total of this stunning display.

Draw on the Spirit for this evidence of a sanctified life. It can build the momentum for the next wave of power. "Till you press the believers to expect this full salvation now," Wesley advises, "you must not look for any revival."[5]

The Spirit also testifies through us with gifts (1 Cor. 12:1–10). If the fruit expresses Jesus' character, gifts demonstrate his ministry. To have a strong witness about Jesus, seek love and eagerly desire spiritual gifts (1 Cor. 14:1).

The first generation of believers spread the gospel with their words but God also testifies. He does it through the signs, wonders, various miracles, and gifts given to these believers (Heb. 2:3–4).

Gifts are the Spirit's main witness in the revival at Azusa Street. The sign gifts brought healing to thousands, the baptism of the Spirit to whole towns, and one of the fastest growing people's movements in history.

Several months into the revival a missionary who visited Azusa Street sends word back from India. "Some of the gifts which have been scarcely heard of in the church for many centuries," he exclaims, "are now being given by the Holy Ghost to simple, unlearned members of the body of Christ. . . . Healings, the gift of tongues, visions and dreams, discernment of spirits, the power to prophecy and to pray the prayer of faith, all have a place in the present revival."[6]

At times the Spirit also witnesses through demonstrations. These are signs in the physical realm indicating God's manifest presence. In the first revival Luke reports a visible fire coming on each believer.

The scriptures record other signs like a dove, clouds, and flames of fire. There's also spiritual intoxication, loss of bodily strength, shaking, altered conscious state, and laughter. At times people witness earth tremors, sighting of angels, and audible sounds from heaven.

In 1960, Duncan Campbell and some students experience one of these demonstrations at an Edinburgh mission school. A report states, "Heavenly music was heard which seemed to fill the room where they were kneeling; it was indescribably beautiful and harmonious, such as no orchestra could symphonise. . . ."[7]

A revival impacting nations is promised at the end at the age. Welcome all the ways the Spirit gives witness. Join these expressions to your own testimony. It draws us toward that final wave of power!

Wallowing on the Dirty Floor

Unfortunately, believers today hesitate over these testimonies of the Spirit. There are different reasons for this misgiving. Some fear there will be abuse, so they dismiss the Spirit's witness altogether. It's a sad fact that leaders do misuse these crowd-gathering works for personal enrichment and promotion. Such corruption of the Spirit's work certainly brings disillusionment.

But to refuse the Spirit's witness because of someone's misuse puts us on dangerous ground. "Is there anything which is so foolish or ridiculous," Martyn Lloyd-Jones asks, "as to dismiss the whole because of the character of a very, very small proportion? If you begin to do that you'll have to dismiss the whole of the New Testament."[8] Turn from fear. Receive the Spirit's testimony and only use it for Jesus' fame.

There's also hesitation because some worry of opposition against the Spirit's witness. I have news for everyone. Opposition usually comes!

"We can have riots without revivals," writes Leonard Ravenhill. "But in the light of the Bible and church history, where can we have revivals without riots?"[9] Demons stir up opposition. They counterattack this way because revival decimates their kingdom like nothing else.

So don't run from the battle. Run to it! We have the advantage. Seek the Spirit's witness until there is an unstoppable advance of holiness, gifts, and signs across the land.

The biggest caution people have is the personal cost. Frankly, it can be significant. The price for revival is full surrender.

A description of Azusa Street shows people paying this price of surrender. It reports, "Proud, well dressed preachers come to 'investigate.' Soon their high looks are replaced with wonder, then conviction comes, and very often you will find them in a short time wallowing on the dirty floor, asking God to forgive them and make them as little children."[10]

How far will you go for another revival? Jesus' method to spread his gospel is still the Spirit's witness. If pride keeps us from this, it's heresy. Not of doctrine, but it's heresy of method.

Lord Jesus Christ, revive me! Give me the Spirit's witness. Evidence your nature, gifts, and signs through me. Make me as a little child crying out to you for revival.

LIVING FORCE

Revival freedom comes to Evan Roberts on September 29, 1904, among the youth in South Wales. A series of meetings is led by the evangelist Seth Joshua, who is asking God for someone to spread revival among the churches. That future leader of the Welsh Revival is Evan Roberts. He describes how the Spirit empowers him to choose wholly for God.

At the close, the Reverend Seth Joshua prayed, and said during his prayer, "Lord, do this, and this . . . and bend us." He did not say, "Oh Lord, bend us." It was the Spirit that put the emphasis for me on "bend us." "That is what you need," said the Spirit to me. And as I went out I prayed, "Oh Lord, bend me."

On the way to the 9:00 [a.m.] meeting, the Reverend Seth Joshua remarked, "We are going to have a wonderful meeting today!" To this I replied, "I feel myself almost bursting." The meeting, having been opened, was handed over to the Spirit. I was conscious that I would have to pray. As one and the other prayed I put the question to the Spirit, "Shall I pray now?" "Wait a while," said He. When others prayed I felt a living force come into my bosom. It held my breath, and my legs shivered and after every prayer I asked, "Shall I now?" The living force grew and grew, and I was almost bursting. . . .

I fell on my knees with my arms over the seat in front of me. . . . I cried, "Bend me! Bend me! Bend us!" Then, "Oh! Oh! Oh! Oh!" and Mrs. Davies said, "Oh wonderful grace!" "Yes," I said, "Oh, wonderful grace!" What bent me was God commending His love. . . .

After I was bent a wave of peace came over me. Oh wonderful, this is life! You've heard it said of joy being felt by men to the tops of their fingers. Yes, it is literally true. And the audience sang, "I hear Thy welcome voice!" And as they sang I thought of the bending at the Judgment Day, and I was filled with compassion for those who would be bent on that day. And I wept.[1]

9

REVIVAL FREEDOM

May God himself, the God of peace, sanctify
you through and through.

—1 THESSALONIANS 5:23

The Most Strategic Freedom

God brings freedom through revivals. Notice
the different freedoms in four of history's great
outpourings. The Second Great Awakening
witnesses at least fifty thousand people set free
from sin every single week over a one-year period.
During the 1984 Argentina Revival, each night large
crowds gather in a designated tent to be set free
from demonic bondage. At Azusa Street countless
sick people are dramatically freed from all kinds of
infirmities. In the British Great Awakening many
believers are set free from sin and selfishness to
live wholly for God.

All these freedoms are important but the final
one where believers are supernaturally empowered to choose for God is very strategic. This is

the experience of sanctification Paul wants for the Thessalonians, and it strengthens a revival more than anything else.

Take the revival in the Hebrides as an example. Before it starts, a few men pray several nights a week in a barn for an awakening. After five months, the Spirit suddenly comes one evening and sanctifies all of them to choose wholly for God. They understand the supernatural empowerment they experience is a prophecy for the coming revival.

"Yes," Duncan Campbell explains, "that was the truth they discovered; revival was coming . . . they were going to see men so supernaturally altered that holiness would characterize every part of their being, body, soul, and spirit."[2]

If the Spirit's empowerment for holy living increases revival's impact, what more should you know about it? As you seek God for the next wave be aware of these facts.

Our Pentecost Has Come

Understand the importance of the Spirit's sanctifying work in past revivals. Among those outpourings you find believers receiving this supernatural empowerment that transforms choices.

The Moravian Revival and First Great Awakening of the early eighteenth century witness many in the church come to know a new level of obedience. But the history-changing moment for the experience is around 1760. That's when John Wesley begins encouraging believers in the British Great Awakening to intentionally go after sanctification instead of hoping it might happen to them.

Wesley proclaims this moral empowerment can be received in a moment of faith. It's at this period in the revival you suddenly notice believers everywhere expecting and experiencing a new capacity to choose wholly for Christ. It comes instantly.

The sanctifying of believers reignites the revival in England and takes America by storm. There, Francis Asbury gets the news that four thousand people are saved on the east cost of Maryland, and a thousand Methodist are supernaturally set free to wholly love God. He declares, "Our Pentecost has come for sanctification."[3]

The Spirit's transformation of believers continues through the revivals of the early nineteenth century. By the time of the Second Great Awakening the popular term for the experience becomes "the baptism of the Holy Spirit" and it surges again.

When you arrive at the end of the nineteenth century a revival is actually named "holiness" because so many believers are being set free from selfish and sinful lives. One American writer at that time exclaims, "I have never seen such an apparent growth in the spirit of holiness. . . ."[4]

The leaders at the Azusa Street Revival in 1906, calling for a new baptism of power evidenced by tongues, warn believers to first seek God for sanctification. They understand this freedom from self-interest is the safest way to wield the power of Pentecost.

Survey the rest of the twentieth century. You find the experience stretching into the middle and even late decades in a number of outpourings. These include the Hebrides and Asbury Revivals.

Now as you seek another wave of revival, consider this question: Do you believe the moral empowerment of believers is necessary for our generation like those of the past?

If your answer is yes, understand it won't happen unless you ask the Spirit to do now what he does over and over again in earlier revivals.

Expect It Now

In order to know what to ask, look at those revivals and see how the Spirit brings believers to this empowerment. Expect what you see for our day.

The Spirit first convicts. Conviction is a supernatural realization that the selfish and sinful choices among believers are wrong. Without it we continue our compromised living and never see the need for the Spirit's moral empowerment.

Sometimes this disturbance is unbearable. During the 1908 Manchurian Revival, believers under conviction strongly object to the closing of a three-hour meeting. They protest, "Please have pity on us and let the meeting go on. For days we haven't been able to sleep."[5]

Whether conviction is that strong or not, ask God to disturb this generation of believers about our compromised living. From conviction the Spirit moves believers to a consecration. Consecration is an intentional decision to want what God wants. It's not attempting by human effort to do what God wants but it's a full surrender of the will to want what he wants. If you're looking for a revival with impact, here's how consecration needs to happen.

God wants you to be dead to sin (Rom. 6:11). You must want and expect this. Without a consecration of your will to God's purposes, you won't choose against sin and selfishness even when the Spirit empowers you. Duncan Campbell says. "The essential nature of sin is my claim to my right to myself. . . . Consecration is my relinquishing of that claim."[6]

A decision to want what God wants even when it goes against your rights to self is only half the consecration. God also wants you alive to his power. You must want and expect it. Without surrendering your will to the Spirit's promptings you won't risk into supernatural power. Determine you want life in the Spirit.

In past revivals, after conviction and consecration, the Spirit then brings to believers faith to ask. If you desire a life with impact, when the Spirit stirs you to believe for sanctifying power, then ask.

How do you ask? As you seek this moral empowerment, John Wesley says, "Expect it by faith, expect it as you are, and expect it now."[7]

Believers of the past use different words when asking. They pray "sanctify me," "fill me," "bend me," and "cleanse me." But the words aren't what matter; it's the expectation. In nearly three hundred years of revivals those petitions of faith see answers. And the answer is fire!

Listen to descriptions of this empowered life that starts in a moment of faith. From the seventeenth century a believer declares, "From about half past ten at night, to about half after midnight, Fire. Forgetfulness of the world and all save God."[8]

"I may say with humility," an eighteenth-century believer shares, "it was as though I was emptied of all evil and filled with heaven and God."[9]

Look at this nineteenth-century person explaining, "All vain ambition, all distracting solicitude, all pride and self-will, and all fear . . . were gone."[10] "Resentment, hostility, hurt feelings—you name it. They all dissolved. Evaporated. Went," is a testimony out of the twentieth century.[11]

Now it's our time to seek this fire. As believers we must ask God to sanctify us so the next revival radically transforms the culture.

Bend the Church

That's one reason "Bend the Church, and save the people" is the slogan of the Welsh Revival. It means people are saved when believers are supernaturally bent to God's will. John Wesley agrees, saying, "wherever the work of sanctification breaks out, the whole work of God prospers."[12]

If it's true the moral empowerment of believers is that important to revival, how does it affect God's move? It protects from temptations. Revival attracts attention, money, and loyalty. These things often tempt leaders and people to pursue self-promotion, self-enrichment, or self-indulgence. But if we relinquish our right to selfish choices and the Spirit moves us to choose for God, revival is protected from pollution by self-centered motives.

Evan Roberts, the popular leader of the Welsh Revival, in a personal letter writes, "I wish no personal following, but only the world for Christ."[13] His intentions and desires are wholly for God. The revival is safe from self-promotion.

Moral empowerment also propels a revival forward by sacrifice. Self-indulgent believers refuse to take the costly actions needed to advance a revival. It can then stall out. But when we consecrate our choices to God's will and we choose sacrifice when the Spirit empowers us, revival keeps surging forward.

Look at the British Great Awakening. Three months into the revival George Whitfield invites John Wesley to preach in the open fields. This outdoor preaching goes against all the order and decency of the Anglican Church. If Wesley chooses to go, it's a deadly blow to his reputation as an Anglican priest. He wrestles with what to do because the Spirit is also moving on his consecrated will.

Wesley reports his choice, saying, "The following Monday at four in the afternoon, I submitted to being more vile, as I thought it, and proclaimed in the highways the glad tidings of salvation . . . to about three thousand people."[14]

A sacrificed reputation propels revival forward!

Do you want a culture-changing revival? Then seek God for an outpouring of sanctifying power. More important, if you personally desire to live wholly for Christ, ask now, by faith and as you are.

Lord Jesus Christ, revive me! Move me to relinquish my right to selfish choices. Empower my will to choose wholly for you. Bring another Holiness Revival.

STRANGE SUPERNATURAL POWER

Revival hope invades the atmosphere over an area named Cane Ridge in 1801. An eyewitness to the scene gives an account of the revival in the backwoods of Kentucky. One estimate of the crowd attending the ten-day encampment is nearly 10 percent of Kentucky's population at the time.

The noise was like the roar of Niagara. The vast sea of human beings seemed to be agitated as if by a storm. I counted seven ministers, all preaching at one time, some on stumps, others in wagons and one standing on a tree which had, in falling, lodged against another. . . . Some of the people were singing, others praying, some crying for mercy in the most piteous accents, while others were shouting most vociferously.

While witnessing these scenes, a peculiarly strange sensation such as I had never felt before came over me. My heart beat tumultuously, my knees trembled, my lips quivered, and I felt as though I must fall to the ground. A strange supernatural power seemed to pervade the entire mass of mind there collected. . . .

I stepped up on a log where I could have a better view of the surging sea of humanity. The scene that then presented itself to my mind was indescribable. At one time I saw at least five hundred swept down in a moment as if a battery of a thousand guns had been opened upon them, and then immediately followed shrieks and shouts that rent the very heavens.[1]

10

REVIVAL HOPE

May the God of hope fill you with all joy
and peace as you trust in him, so that you
may overflow with hope by the power of the
Holy Spirit.

—Romans 15:13

Tasting the Future

Our hope is like no other. Its vibrancy overcomes
life's difficulties. This hope is about Jesus' return.
In revival it flows so strong that even unbelievers
become fascinated by it.

How is this possible? Does the Spirit suddenly
inspire people to buy books about the earthly return
and reign of Jesus? That would be informative, but
it's not how it works. Hope isn't a knowledge you
get through books. It's an experience you receive
through the Spirit.

Revival hope is an experiential taste of what's
coming in our future. Jonathan Edwards believes
these experiences actually move history closer
to this future God has pledged. He says, "the

Father implements this pledge in part by successive outpourings of the Spirit, which prove the realities of Christ's coming kingdom to a skeptical world. . . ."[2]

Revival hope proves the realities of Christ's coming kingdom by allowing us to experience those realities, but it's only in part. Revival is a community-wide sampling of the age to come.

In the Moravian Revival of 1727 a person explains how people left the meeting "not knowing whether they belonged to earth or had already gone to heaven."[3] This confusion comes because they taste Christ's future reign when heaven draws closer to earth.

Revival hope is experiential proof of our future with Jesus Christ. It's not a fact you learn. It's living! You actually taste what's ahead. Here are some samples of the coming age you encounter in part.

Divine Magnetism

Paul identifies one aspect of our future in Isaiah. These prophecies speak of a time when Israel's king reigns on earth and the nations rally to him (see Romans 15:12; Isaiah 11:10). The physical presence of Messiah is so magnetic the peoples of the earth are drawn to Zion where he reigns.

During the Asbury Revival, Steve Seamands reports a strange drawing effect in the auditorium. "The power of God was so present and so real that time itself seemed to collapse. It was almost as if we were in a suspended state of reality and people would sit in Hughes for hour upon hour and it seemed like only seconds."[4]

This radical encounter of the coming age overrides the distractions of this age. "Time itself seems to collapse" as attention is pulled to Jesus Christ who one day will rule the earth. "We may be sure that when God begins to work the people will be there," explains Arthur Wallis, "drawn not by invitation or persuasion, but by that divine magnetism that operates in revival."[5]

The power pulls and holds people. "When I entered I felt some mysterious power seize me," says a seeker in revival, "impelling me to confess my sins, and it was only with the utmost difficulty I could drag myself away."[6]

Drawing power can be tasted personally before it's ever known in revival. God offers an inner experience of what's in store after our resurrection. Paul says, "Christ in you," bringing with him the hope of all the glorious things to come (Col. 1:27).[7]

This heartfelt undertow from another age is described by Charles Finney. He reports, "At this time it seemed as if my soul was wedded to Christ in a sense in which I had never had any thought or conception of before."[8]

As revival comes on Northampton, Sarah Edwards personally reports, "The presence of God was so near and so real that I seemed scarcely conscious of anything else."[9]

Expect divine magnetism in your heart through the Spirit's power. But also ask for the next revival when others rally to Jesus like the nations will in the coming age.

Unspeakable Joy

Revival is a taste of what is experienced after resurrection. These samples of your future are love and peace, but one of the most striking is joy. Joy is not happiness. It is a preview of the sheer exhilaration we'll know in the coming age.

Peter writes to a group of suffering believers experiencing something beyond their circumstances. It's an indescribable foretaste of the joy when Jesus reigns on earth (1 Peter 1:8). The Thessalonians, also under the persecution of this age, sample this reality of the coming age (1 Thess. 1:6).

The revival in England under Wesley and Whitfield explodes in a little gathering on New Year's 1739. "About three in the morning, as we were continuing instant in prayer," John Wesley reports, "the power of God came mightily upon us, insomuch that many cried out for exulting joy, and many fell to the ground."[10]

Whether joy knocks you down or moves sweetly across your soul, press into it. Do it by rejoicing. Find ways to manifest what you feel. When you do, it secures, increases, and spreads joy.

One eyewitness to the unspeakable joy in the 1851 Welsh Revival reports, "Such excitement, such jumping and exulting I never saw either before or since! Old men and women clasping each other's hands and leaping like roe deer. . . . Some weeping, some singing, others exulting and very many doing this while 'leaping and praising God.' This was a meeting to be remembered for ever!"[11]

A church official in England condemns another joyous group in Wales calling them "jumpers."

Roland Hill, one of the revivalists, responds to this name-calling. He declares that the English might yell "Jumpers! Jumpers!" at the Welsh, but the Welsh can justly yell at the English, "Sleepers! Sleepers!"[12]

Maybe you sample joy but don't rejoice. You're sleeping instead of jumping. Wake up and express your joy! If you want revival, give yourself to the slightest taste of your future.

Taking the Devil by Surprise

Paul says the Holy Spirit is the Spirit of wisdom and revelation (Eph. 1:17–19). That's because the Spirit gives wisdom that's not of this age. It's most prominent in revival.

The wisdom of our age calls for a strong leader but the wisdom of revival cries out for God's presence. This age attempts to gather people by marketing. Revival draws people by divine magnetism. The ways of the world warn us not to offend. The ways of revival say God is God even if people don't understand.

"There is no mightier corrective to worldly methods in Christian service," writes Arthur Wallis, "than a heaven-sent revival."[13]

Peter Cartwright is a Methodist circuit rider saved through the influence of the Cane Ridge Revival. Whether he goes in a home, a church, or a camp meeting, he doesn't wait for revival, he brings it!

Cartwright stays at an inn overnight in eastern Kentucky where the gospel is unknown. That evening he goes downstairs to observe the noisy dancing and drinking. A young lady out of courtesy asks the stranger to dance. Prompted by the Holy Spirit, he joins her and goes to the dance floor. Before the fiddler starts, Cartwright explains to the crowd his desire to see God's favor come on everyone. Still holding the young lady's hand, he kneels and asks God to show up.

The power of God immediately hits! The young girl falls to the floor crying for God's mercy. The fiddler runs away shouting, "What does this mean?" Some flee but many stay and come to the Lord. The meeting goes into the next day and evening. Cartwright eventually plants a church there. The innkeeper is its leader and several of the men become Methodist circuit riders.

The wisdom of revival doesn't fit the thinking of this age. Cartwright says of the incident, "Surely, in all human wisdom, it was out of season, but I had, from some cause or other, a strong impression on my mind, from the beginning to the end of this affair, (if it is ended) that I should succeed by taking the devil by surprise. . . ."

Then Cartwright turns his guns on us. "In this agency of the Holy Spirit of God I have been a firm believer for more than fifty-four years, and I do firmly believe that if the ministers of the present day had more of the unction or baptismal fire of the Holy Ghost prompting their ministerial efforts, we should succeed much better than we do. . . ."[14]

Ask for the Spirit's strategy and taste the wisdom of the coming age. It outflanks the wisdom of this present age every time.

Maybe revival should be called "previval." Revival is experiencing the life of our past; previval is experiencing the life of our future. Seek another wave that rolls over our nation from the deep waters of the coming age.

Lord Jesus Christ, revive me! Give me greater tastes of the coming age with you. Pour out your Spirit until I see this hope overflow on others. Do what it takes to shake the nation.

DIVINE PRESENCE

Revival worldview becomes the instant mind-set for William Haslam on October 19, 1851. He is an unconverted parson serving the Baldhu Hill parish in Cornwall, England. Through his congregation's prayers he is converted while preaching a sermon! That very day revival starts.

In the providence of God, my conversion was the beginning of a great revival in my parish which continued without much interruption for nearly three years. At some periods during that time there was a greater power of the Divine presence, and consequently more manifest results, than at others; but all along there were conversions of sinners or restoration of backsliders every week—indeed almost every day!

During the revival, the outpouring of the Spirit of God was manifest and unmistakable, and was seen in various ways. Every week, almost every day, we heard of some remarkable dream or striking visions.

. . . We could not help people being stricken down, neither could they help it themselves; often the most unlikely persons were overcome and became excited, and persons naturally quiet and retiring proved most noisy and demonstrative. However, it was our joy to see permanent results afterwards, which more than reconciled us to any amount of inconvenience we had felt at the time.

In the school-room, evening by evening, the Lord wrought a great work, and showed forth His power in saving many souls. I have seldom read of any remarkable manifestations in revivals the counterpart of which I did not witness in the room; and I saw some things the which I have never heard of as taking place anywhere else.[1]

11

REVIVAL WORLDVIEW

... a partial hardening has come upon Israel,
until the fullness of the Gentiles has come in.
And in this way all Israel will be saved ...

—Romans 11:25–26 esv

Standing in the Last of the Last

Our view of revival shapes how we live. If revival
is a pointless demonstration of religious fervor,
we live to avoid it. If it is an emergency fix for the
church, we sometimes seek it but only if things
get bad. But if revival moves history toward Jesus'
return, we do everything we can to live for the
next wave. That's when it's no longer a view but a
worldview.

Peter has a revival worldview. He indicates the
outpouring at Pentecost begins a unique period
of revival. It culminates as Joel predicts in a
worldwide outpouring before the day of the Lord
(Acts 2:16–21; 3:19–20).

"The fullness of the Gentiles" is how Paul designates a final revival (Rom. 11:25 ESV). He lives to realize more waves until the final one that turns Israel to Jesus.

D. M. Patton declares, "that while the Christian centuries are 'the last days,' and Pentecost began the wonder, we today, standing in the last of the last, are on the edge of a second and more tremendous upheaval of the Holy Spirit."[2]

Many today live like the "last of the last" is a time of despair. They see nothing but the prophesied increase of evil at the end of the age. But these prophecies actually support the revival worldview. Evil's increase isn't Satan's attack. It's his desperate counterattack against an unstoppable wave of power.

Wake up and shake off despair. We play a part in bringing this great revival. Here's how a revival worldview changes the way you live.

Bringing the Age to Come

It stirs you to always seek more. Look at Paul. He wants believers to be "filled to the measure of all the fullness of God" (Eph. 3:19). That sounds very much like the final revival.

A revival worldview grips you to seek more. Richard Owen Robert says revival praying is "when extraordinary seeking of an extraordinary outpouring becomes extraordinarily earnest. . . ."[3] Such praying is important because it forges us into determined seekers of more. The final revival will be the biggest "more" the world has ever known. God wants a people that will not relent until they get it.

In 1748 Jonathan Edwards and other North American pastors receive correspondence from the pastors of Scotland. It's an invitation to join them in seven years of praying for the final worldwide revival. Using Zechariah's prophecy, Edwards shows how this strategy could bring that long-awaited outpouring.

Obviously, the plan doesn't bring the final revival but before you write off their prayer effort, consider this. Those believers become one of the links in a chain of prayers stretching into the Cane Ridge Revival some fifty years later. Even if a prayer effort doesn't bring the final wave, it can unleash the next one.

"Every great revival has come to the church," says David Bryant, "when God has ignited a 'critical mass' of Christians who are determined to look to God for revival, and nowhere else, and to do so until revival comes."[4]

In other words, determined seekers of more realize the next wave. So here's the question: Are you this kind of seeker? Maybe you think, *I don't even know how to make myself a determined seeker*. I've got news for you. You can't! But you can pray yourself into one.

If you want more, God puts that desire there. So start by asking Jesus to revive you. As you experience more of God's power, don't stop. You're in this until God's greatest "more" is here.

At the revival's highest point in Wales, Evan Roberts takes time out and seeks God for more. He goes away a whole week, never leaving his room. Roberts won't even allow the more of the Welsh Revival keep him from seeking more.

Be a determined seeker. When you experience increase, go for more because God's more can't be exhausted.

Remarkable Communications of the Spirit

The worldview of revival inspires you to not only seek but receive more. Jonathan Edwards says, "From the fall of man to our day the work of redemption in its effect has mainly been carried on by remarkable communications of the Spirit of God."[5] These remarkable Spirit encounters bring a greater obedience to Jesus.

Receivers of more welcome encounters with God. They always lead the charge toward the new thing God is doing while everyone else admires what God has done. In the Congo Revival of 1953, the people risk into powerful and unfamiliar encounters of the Spirit. Sharing how the work spread one missionary explains, "We are convinced that wherever there is a genuine desire for revival and a willingness to accept what God sends, without any heart reservations, God will not pass them by."[6]

Since revivals are progressive waves, be ready to encounter more of God. Please understand, this isn't a call for more dramatic or weird experiences; it's an invitation to the "remarkable communications" of the Spirit exalting Jesus in this hour.

As you receive don't become an isolated mystic. Revival is corporate. God wants Jesus' character manifest among a people. Reaching the "whole measure of the fullness of Christ" (Eph. 4:13), comes through unity with others in an encounter with the Son of God.

Also, don't check out of daily life in an obsessive pursuit for encounters. The setting of the extraordinary work of God is our ordinary life, or revival has no meaning.

Charles Finney warns that revivals die when "the Church gets *exhausted* by labors . . . multitudes of Christians neglect to eat and sleep at the proper hours and let the excitement run away with them so they become exhausted. . . ."[7]

The revival in Wales lasts a year and a half, impacting much of the nation. It's a wild and exhausting run that brings a young receiver of more, Evan Roberts, to physical and mental depletion. He goes and remains in seclusion after the revival.

Before his death at seventy-one, he creates a pamphlet showing he is still receiving more. It's called *Hours in the Presence of God* and gives a wonderful piece of advice. It says, "Rest well in order not to miss the guidance of the Spirit toward and during times of prayer."[8]

If you embrace a revival worldview, learn to rest well so you won't miss the Spirit's guidance toward and during times of revival.

The Power of Signs and Miracles

This worldview causes you to also take more. Prophecy shows a future generation taking more of heaven and earth than at any other time in history. These will be the ones who push into the final revival.

More earth is taken in the largest harvest of people ever known. John sees martyrs at the end of the age entering heaven out of a great harvest on earth (Rev. 7:9–14). James speaks of waiting for a latter rain that increases the fruit of harvest before Jesus comes (James 5:7–8). Paul tells of a harvest among nations that even brings Israel to a jealousy for what the Spirit is doing (Rom. 11:25–27).

But the harvest doesn't happen by itself. Believers take more earth because they're taking more heaven.

Paul makes much of his ministry that brings some Jews to Jesus. He sees it as a small-scale example of how the final revival helps turn Israel to Jesus (Rom. 11:11, 13–14). Later he describes his ministry as "the power of signs and miracles, through the power of the Spirit" (Rom. 15:18–19).

The revival at the end of the age is Paul's ministry magnified a billion times over. Israel and other nations will be fascinated by these supernatural signs of Jesus' Lordship.

At Azusa Street people take more earth. They demolish the demonic stronghold of racism, becoming one of the most ethnically diverse meetings in the country. Within months, missionaries are spreading out to harvest the earth. More than a hundred years later, nearly 700 million believers claim their faith flows from the fount of Azusa.

The incredible taking of earth is due to a massive taking of heaven. The revival sees the release of healing, tongues, miracles, and supernatural gifts. Eyewitnesses speak of a visible glory cloud in the old warehouse and occasional sightings of fire over the building. These are signs of heaven breaking into earth.

Just a few days before this supernatural eruption of power, Frank Bartleman pens these prophetic words: "And now, once more, at the very end of the age, God calls. . . . A final call, a worldwide revival. Then judgment upon the whole world. Some tremendous event is about to transpire. . . ."[9]

It turns out that "tremendous event" isn't the final revival but it is the next one. Those simple people do it! They take so much of heaven that the wave of Azusa still floods the earth.

Now comes our turn. It's time to go for the next revival. Who knows, it may be the last one. But whether it is or not, every wave brings us closer to Jesus' return. And when he comes, God's tide of glory then covers the earth as waters cover the sea.

Lord Jesus Christ, revive me! Move me to seek more, receive more, and take more. Make me faithful even into the next revival. May it be the one that brings your return!

12

WHAT'S AHEAD?

The past has not exhausted the possibilities nor the demands for doing great things for God. The Church that is dependent on its past history for its miracles of power and grace is a fallen Church.

—E. M. Bounds[1]

Revival Rising should leave you asking yourself one question: *What's ahead for me?* That's because this book isn't simply a review of past revivals. These narratives, stories, and words are written to stir expectation for your future.

If you sense a stirring, what you feel could be much more than excitement about the possibility of revival. The Spirit often uses revival testimonies to get us praying. He's always building momentum for another surge of power.

Can you hear the Spirit calling you? If so, you must decide if you are going to wade into the prayer currents of God's next wave. To encourage you in making an affirmative response, consider these three truths.

The Priority of Revival

God's next wave is something you *ought* to pursue. It's not just a good idea. Revival is God's great strategy for these last days.

God wants to give people a sample of what they hunger for in their lives. Whether they know it or not, people are longing for Jesus and his kingdom. The greatest taste of that kingdom this side of Jesus' return comes in revival.

Settle it, once and for all. You are to go after revival so your generation gets a sample of Jesus' coming kingdom. If you're in a group, a church, or in agreement with just one other believer, start praying for God's next wave of power. It's something you're called to do.

The Possibility of Revival

Another revival is not just something you *ought* to pursue. It's something you *can* go after.

Maybe you're not sure of that. "My prayers won't ever bring a revival," you protest. "I'm no John Wesley or Evan Roberts. I'm not one of those great men or women of God who obtains revival through prayer."

Look again at the "great men and women of God." Notice before the revival comes they are as simple and unknown as you are. In history it's the nameless, faceless people who break through with prayer.

Think of it. You can start going after revival today. You can do it because you are as ordinary and unknown as all those who have ever prayed for revival and got it.

It doesn't matter how the Spirit is inspiring you to pray. It can be through the testimonies in this book, concern for your culture, or reports of a distant revival. What does matter is the Spirit inspires you to pray because revival is obtainable by those who are faithful.

The Urgency of Revival

But that's not all. You not only *ought* and *can* pray for revival, you *must*.

On the negative side, you must seek it because spiritual power diminishes over time. Revival is not a magic bullet. It's a wave that lasts for a season. But during that time the surge of power floods us with salvation, fullness, joy, and transformation. Every generation needs a revival.

On the positive side, you must pursue revival because it pushes history toward the return of Jesus. Since each successive wave moves the tide of God's purpose to its ultimate fulfillment, the next revival wave must always be in sight.

Revival is not an option or a fad for religious fanatics. It is the biggest taste of God's coming kingdom we can sample in this present age. For that reason alone, you must seek another wave surging over your generation.

Are you still undecided? Charles Finney, the great revivalist, has three penetrating questions to help you determine if you really want to obey God's call.

- *If God should ask you this moment, by an audible voice from heaven, "Do you want a revival?" would you dare to say: "Yes"?*
- *If He were to ask: "Are you willing to make the sacrifices?" would you answer: "Yes"?*
- *And if He said: "When shall it begin?" would you answer: "Let it begin tonight—let it begin here—let it begin in my heart NOW"?*[2]

APPENDIX 1

This list is not a catalogue of all revivals or the most influential ones, but it describes the majority of revivals mentioned in *Revival Rising*. The description is brief so it omits many important events and persons surrounding each outpouring.

The Moravian Revival (1727–1739)

Moravians and other religious refugees flee to Germany, finding asylum on the estate of Count Nicholas von Zinzendorf in Saxony. Doctrinal differences create disunity among the people so Zinzendorf calls the arguing refugees to pray. On August 13, 1727, three days after God's presence is felt in a prayer service, revival comes in power at a communion service. Being transformed from religious bickering to unity and joy, the people quickly organize a relay of continuous prayer watches to secure and increase the work of the Spirit. Within weeks another wave of revival comes on the children holding their own prayer gatherings. Moravians begin to fan out over the world as missionaries, even bringing two English brothers, John and Charles Wesley, to salvation and influencing the British Great Awakening. Their continuous prayer watches last a hundred years, spreading salvation, holiness of life, prayer, and the nearness of Christ.

The American Great Awakening (1734–1760)

In December of 1734, Jonathan Edwards sees the spark of revival one Sunday through five or six conversions at his Northampton church in Massachusetts, so he calls the people to start praying. Six months later three hundred people are saved, and within two years Edwards reports that God's manifest presence is felt over the entire town. The revival quickly spreads throughout the Northeast by the preaching of Edwards and three brothers named Tennent. It advances again in 1745, when George Whitfield's visit to America triggers another surge in Northampton and other communities. Salvation for many unbelievers and a deep experiential encounter with God's love among believers characterize the revival. Lasting twenty-six years, the awakening transforms the moral character of the American people and prepares them for the miraculous birth of their nation.

The British Great Awakening (1739–1791)

On January 1, 1739, John and Charles Wesley, George Whitfield, and other friends are gathered in prayer with a group of Moravians when the Spirit overwhelms them with revival power. Six months later John Wesley and George Whitfield are preaching in the open fields to crowds of fifteen thousand or more from all levels of society. The revival literally shakes individuals with God's power until all of England is influenced. George Whitfield travels to America thirteen times, sparking revival through his preaching in both countries. John Wesley secures and spreads the revival for the next fifty years by organizing his people into small weekly cell groups. The revival is characterized by countless salvations and believers entering a life of holiness through an encounter with God's perfect love. Many believe England's radical transformation through this awakening saves it from a bloody revolution like the one in France.

The Cane Ridge Revival (1801–1830)

Barton Stone, a Presbyterian minister, witnesses a work of the Spirit at a small outdoor camp meeting in Logan County, Kentucky. A year later in 1801, at Cane Ridge in Bourbon County, he holds a camp meeting that explodes on the American scene as the largest, most spectacular revival in the 1800s. The attendance, estimated as high as twenty-five thousand people, is made up of non-believers and believers from all denominations. The Presbyterians end up tossing away this revival hot potato with its unusual physical manifestations. The Methodists and some Baptists pick it up and start running with it. Over the next thirty years the camp meeting becomes an effective delivery system for revival, transforming many parts of the nation, particularly the South. The revival is marked by countless salvations, experiences of heart holiness, and strong manifestations of the Spirit.

The American Second Great Awakening (1824–1860)

Three revival streams converge to become another American Great Awakening, peaking in 1859, with a million people converted in that one year. The first stream is Charles Finney, a lawyer saved and filled with the Spirit on October 10, 1821. His powerful experience in the Holy Spirit launches him as a revivalist in the northeastern United States from 1824 to 1834, culminating with a move of God in Rochester, New York, that spawns revivals in fifteen hundred towns. He gives some lectures on revival and later publishes them in a book, increasing hunger for revival and triggering many outpourings over the world.

The second revival stream is a Methodist couple, Walter and Phoebe Palmer, who preach an experience of holiness through the baptism of the Holy Spirit. They help bring revival to Canada in 1857, and in portions of the United States and England.

The third stream is Jeremiah C. Lanphier of New York, who starts a prayer meeting with other businessmen in 1859. After a market crash in October, the noon prayer meeting goes daily, and similar prayer meetings spring up in cities across America, with some having attendance of six thousand. New York sees fifty thousand converts and the prayer meetings spark as many as two thousand local revivals across the country. The Second Great Awakening is marked by many salvations, believers being filled with the Holy Spirit for a holy life and God's manifest presence, which is actually felt by sailors on ships entering the New York Harbor.

The Holiness Revival (1867–1894)

Three Methodist pastors—J. A. Wood, John Inskip, and William Osborn—determine to revive the camp-meeting movement as a delivery system for the waning holiness experience as preached by John Wesley and earlier Methodists. In July 1867, their first camp meeting calls people to salvation and believers to the baptism of the Spirit for holy living. Over the next fifteen years, fifty-two holiness camp meetings spring up primarily in Methodist circles, with some attracting more than twenty thousand people. The revival spreads from the northern states to the war-torn South and then to England, influencing there many groups like the Salvation Army and the Keswick Convention. By 1880 the revival is spawning Holiness denominations, evangelists, literature, and schools all over the country. The Holiness Revival manifests salvations, baptisms of the Spirit for holy living, healings, and a tangible sense of God's experiential love.

The Welsh Revival (1904–1906)

Evan Roberts prays for and receives the Holy Spirit's fullness with an intense compassion for the unbelievers of Wales. Holding a meeting at his home church on October 31, 1904, the Spirit comes in power. Evan starts traveling with a team of young adults, having countless revival meetings marked by prayer and worship. By January 1905, seventy thousand conversions are reported. Over the next three years, the news and visitors from the revival spread revival to at least twenty-two other nations. At the time the population of Wales is a million, and one estimate places the number of conversions at two hundred and fifty thousand. The revival is marked by many salvations, believers being filled with the Spirit, joyous worship, intense prayer, and a tangible sense of God's presence.

The Azusa Street Revival (1906–1909)

Inspired by the Welsh Revival, hundreds of people pray for revival in Los Angeles, California, when William Seymour, a black Holiness preacher, arrives in town from Texas. On April 9, 1906, he and seven others in a home meeting suddenly fall to the ground, speaking with other tongues. Attendance increases so quickly, the gathering is moved to an old warehouse on Azusa Street, where the meetings last through the days and into the nights. News of the tongues and other signs of power bring trainloads of people from across the United States. Within six months, missionaries go out from Azusa Street, while visitors scatter over the country spreading the same experiences. The revival peaks in three years, but spawns a movement still causing transformation in many nations. Countless salvations, baptisms of the Spirit with tongues, healings, holy living, and manifestations of the Spirit characterize the revival.

The Hebrides Revival (1949–1952)

In Scotland's Outer Hebrides two elderly sisters, Peggy and Christine Smith, continually praying for a move of God, get a vision of the empty churches packed with young people. As the Spirit begins to manifest in their local church's prayer gathering, the minister invites Duncan Campbell to the island to hold meetings. When he arrives the church is packed with people drawn from many of the surrounding villages. The meeting goes late into the night, with people falling prostrate and crying for forgiveness. The revival spreads to other villages, where a tangible sense of God's presence is felt and heavenly music is heard on two occasions. Campbell continues his ministry for the next two years, with many of the converted becoming ministers and missionaries. The prayer meetings have larger crowds than the public worship services and bring a revival of countless salvations, baptisms of the Spirit for holy living, deliverances, and a strong sense of God's presence.

The Asbury College Revival (1970)

On February 3, 1970, in a chapel service at Asbury College, a Kentucky school founded through the Holiness Revival, a student gives a spontaneous testimony, causing a rush of students seeking salvation and full surrender. God's presence fills the auditorium, bringing a greater response of students and leading to the suspension of all classes. The next few days see hundreds of visitors from surrounding states, while the students go out across the country spreading revival to churches and colleges. The chapel service in the college auditorium continues nonstop for 185 hours through eight days and seven nights, becoming one of the longest uninterrupted revival meetings. By summer, more than 130 colleges, Bible schools, seminaries, and countless churches experience revival. The revival is marked by salvations, baptisms in the Holy Spirit for holy living, testimonies, and God's manifest presence.

The Toronto Revival (1994–2006)

After experiencing an empowerment of the Holy Spirit, Randy Clarke, on January 20, 1994, shares his testimony with 120 people at a Vineyard church in Toronto. The Holy Spirit comes in power on the congregation of John Arnott, with people falling to the floor, crying, and laughing. As word spreads about the unusual manifestations so many visitors come, the church moves to a larger building that accommodates a flow of hundreds of thousands of people flying in from all over the world. The revival spreads into North America, England, Mozambique, and many more nations. It spawns a new network of renewal churches and ministry schools over the world. Salvations, healings, releases from oppression, powerful manifestations of the Spirit, and a tangible sense of God's love characterize the revival.

APPENDIX 2
PRAYING TOGETHER FOR THE NEXT WAVE

Consider gathering others to pray for revival using *Revival Rising*. Take twelve consecutive weeks, commit to come together, and pray through each chapter. The exercises below are meant to focus your time of prayer together.

One exercise is a prayer focus taken from a past *revival* described in the narrative before each chapter. Another exercise gives a prayer focus from the portion of the *Bible* quoted at the beginning of each chapter. The next one brings a prayer focus that's *personal* and drawn from the chapter's topic. The final exercise focuses on a specific *petition* from the prayer at the end of each chapter. Everyone's response to this final exercise is important to prime the time of praying.

Don't try doing all four exercises each week. Do some, but carefully guard half your time to pray together for God's next wave.

Week One—Revival Power

1. *Revival Focus:* What do you think Duncan Campbell means when he finds the "community

alive with an awareness of God," and how do you pray for it?

2. *Bible Focus:* In 2 Thessalonians 1:11–12 when Paul says that God fulfills our good resolve and works of faith by his power, how does that relate to the way you pray for revival power?

3. *Personal Focus:* Give some ways you think spiritual energy is diminishing today and how revival power could change it.

4. *Petition Focus:* Share which petition in the closing prayer of the first chapter speaks most to you and why.

Week Two—Revival Life

1. *Revival Focus:* From the opening narrative, discuss some of the ways revival life is described during the Asbury Revival and how to seek God for these realities.

2. *Bible Focus:* Paul prays in Ephesians 3:16–17 that believers will be strengthened with power by the Spirit in their "inner being." How should his prayer influence the way you pray for revival?

3. *Personal Focus:* What do you think it means to pray that Jesus' presence would excite the church?

4. *Petition Focus:* Which petition in the closing prayer of chapter 2 stands out to you and why?

Week Three—Revival Culture

1. *Revival Focus:* In the opening narrative, the writer describes the Spirit influencing the camp-meeting

culture with power. How can we pray for this influence in our church culture today?

2. *Bible Focus:* In Galatians 3:3 Paul says that believers are foolish to begin in the Spirit and then turn to human effort. Share examples of human effort we depend on instead of the Spirit.

3. *Personal Focus:* Share anything about the Holy Spirit that makes you cautious.

4. *Prayer Focus:* Which petition in the closing prayer of chapter 3 stands out most to you and why?

Week Four—Revival Experience

1. *Revival Focus:* From the opening narrative, why do you think Joseph Kemp says the awakening isn't "transient" but "abides"?

2. *Bible Focus:* In Ephesians 3:19 how do you think we pray for the knowledge of love surpassing knowledge?

3. *Personal Focus:* Share a time God taught you something through a personal spiritual experience and how you believe you can seek God for more experiences like that one.

4. *Prayer Focus:* Which petition in the closing prayer speaks most to you and why?

Week Five—Revival Glory

1. *Revival Focus:* In the opening narrative, why do you think manifestations like the "glory fits" sometimes show up in revivals?

2. *Bible Focus:* Paul says in 2 Corinthians 3:11–12 that we have a greater glory. How do you think we should pray for God's manifest glory?

3. *Personal Focus:* Do you feel any reluctance about revival and, if so, how can you ask God for help to overcome this hesitation?

4. *Prayer Focus:* Which petition in the closing prayer of chapter 5 speaks most to you and why?

Week—Revival Love

1. *Revival Focus:* What do you think Jonathan Edwards means in the opening narrative when he says believers had their "religious affections raised"?

2. *Bible Focus:* In Romans 5:5 Paul says the Spirit pours out God's love in our hearts. How do you think the Spirit's outpouring of love relates to revival?

3. *Personal Focus:* Share about your most significant encounter with God's love and how you will pray for more of these experiences.

4. *Prayer Focus:* Which petition in the closing prayer speaks most to you and why?

Week Seven—Revival Humility

1. *Revival Focus:* What do you think Frank Bartleman means in the opening narrative by saying "no pride" was at Azusa Street?

2. *Bible Focus:* Paul says in 2 Corinthians 4:7 that we should show that "all-surpassing power" belongs to God. How do you think these words

should influence the revival you're asking God to bring?
3. *Personal Focus:* Share your biggest battle with pride.
4. *Prayer Focus:* Which petition in the closing prayer in chapter 7 speaks most to you and why?

Week Eight—Revival Witness

1. *Revival Focus:* What does C. G. Bevington show you about praying for the Spirit's witness?
2. *Bible Focus:* Tell what you think Paul means in 1 Thessalonians 1:5 by the gospel coming "with power, with the Holy Spirit and with deep conviction." How do you think this affects your praying for revival?
3. *Personal Focus:* Share any hesitation you have about receiving the Spirit's witness.
4. *Prayer Focus:* Which petition in the closing prayer speaks most to you and why?

Week Nine—Revival Freedom

1. *Revival Focus:* In the opening narrative, what do you think Evan Roberts means by a "living force" coming into him?
2. *Bible Focus:* In 1 Thessalonians 5:23 Paul desires God to sanctify believers "through and through." How should his desire influence what you should pray for in revival?
3. *Personal Focus:* Do you think it is possible to live wholly for Christ every day and why?

4. *Prayer Focus:* Which petition in the closing prayer in chapter 9 speaks most to you and why?

Week Ten—Revival Hope

1. *Revival Focus:* Reading the narrative about the Cane Ridge Revival, why do you think the revival is so dramatic and do you think we need something like it again?
2. *Bible Focus:* In Romans 15:13 Paul speaks about hope overflowing "by the power of the Holy Spirit." How should that influence what you pray for in a coming revival?
3. *Personal Focus:* Share how you can better express the joy of your salvation.
4. *Prayer Focus:* Which petition in the closing prayer speaks most to you and why?

Week Eleven—Revival Worldview

1. *Revival Focus:* In the narrative, what do you think William Haslam means when he says the Spirit's outpouring was "manifest and unmistakable"?
2. *Bible Focus:* Paul says in Romans 11:25–26 all Israel will be saved when the fullness of the Gentiles comes in. How do you think you should pray for the fullness of the Gentiles?
3. *Personal Focus:* In what way is God calling you to take more of heaven?
4. *Prayer Focus:* Which petition in the closing prayer speaks most to you and why?

Week Twelve—What's Ahead?

1. *Personal Focus:* Share how you answer Finney's three questions at the end of this chapter and why.
2. *Prayer Focus:* Discuss together how you will continue to pray for revival, and then pray for each other.

NOTES

Preface: A Word of Caution

1. Mathew Backholer, *Revival Answers, True and False Revival, Genuine or Counterfeit* (United Kingdom: ByFaith Media, 2012), 91.
2. James Burns, *Revivals: Their Laws and Leaders* (Grand Rapids, MI: Baker, 1960), 23.

Chapter One: Revival Power

1. Duncan Campbell, *The Price and Power of Revival* (Fort Washington, PA: Christian Literature Crusade, 1962), 66–67.
2. Mathew Backholer, *Revival Fires and Awakenings: Thirty-Six Visitations of the Holy Spirit: A Call to Holiness, Prayer and Intercession for the Nations* (United Kingdom: ByFaith Media, 2012), 137.
3. James Burns, *Revivals: Their Laws and Leaders* (Grand Rapids, MI: Baker, 1960), 32.
4. Winkie Pratney, *Revival: Principles to Change the World* (Springdale, PA: Whitaker House, 1984), 15.
5. S. B. Shaw, *The Great Revival in Wales* (Pensacola, FL: Christian Life Books, 2002), 47.
6. Frank Bartleman, *Azusa Street: An Eyewitness Account* (Alachua, FL: Bridge-Logos, 1980), 67.
7. James Burns, *Revivals*, 21.
8. Backholer, *Revival Fires and Awakenings*, 16.
9. Charles Haddon Spurgeon, "The Story of God's Mighty Acts," a sermon preached July 17, 1859, http://revival-library.org/index.php/resources-menu/revival-sermons/the-story-of-god-s-mighty-acts.
10. Charles Finney, *Lectures on Revivals of Religion* (Westwood, NJ: Fleming H. Revell Co.), 35–48.

11. Gilbert Egerton, *Flame of God: Distinctives of Revival* (Belfast, Northern Ireland: Ambassador Productions, 1987), 84–85.
12. Backholer, *Revival Fires and Awakenings*, 97.

Chapter Two: Revival Life

1. Robert E. Coleman, ed., *One Divine Moment: The Asbury Revival* (Old Tappan, NJ: Fleming H. Revell Company, 1970), 27–43.
2. Gilbert Egerton, *Flame of God: Distinctives of Revival* (Belfast, Northern Ireland: Ambassador Productions, 1987), 77.
3. Norman P. Grubb, *Continuous Revival: The Secret of Victorious Living* (Fort Washington, PA: Christian Literature Crusade, 1997), 6.
4. James Burns, *Revival: Their Laws and Leaders* (Grand Rapids, MI: Baker, 1960), 28.
5. "America's Great Revivals: The Story of Spiritual Revival in the United States, 1734–1899" *Sunday Magazine, Inc.*, 33.
6. Stephen Olford, *Heart Cry for Revival* (Fern, Scotland, UK: Christian Focus, 2005), 138–39.
7. Burns, *Revival*, 23.
8. Charles Finney, *Lectures on Revivals of Religion* (Westwood, NJ: Fleming H. Revell Co.), 529.
9. Jonathan Edwards, *Jonathan Edwards: On Revival* (Carlisle, PA: The Banner of Truth Trust, 1995), 151.
10. Finney, *Lectures on Revivals of Religion*, 2.
11. Dennis F. Kinlaw, *Prayer: Bearing the World as Jesus Did* (Anderson, IN: Francis Asbury Press, 2013), 97.
12. Mathew Backholer, *Revival Fires and Awakenings: Thirty-Six Visitations of the Holy Spirit: A Call to Holiness, Prayer and Intercession for the Nations* (United Kingdom: ByFaith Media, 2012), 151.

Chapter Three: Revival Culture

1. Adam Wallace, *A Modern Pentecost* (The Methodist Home Journal Publishing House, 1873), 121–22.
2. Gilbert Egerton, *Flame of God: Distinctives of Revival* (Belfast: Northern Ireland: Ambassador Productions, 1987), 64.

3. J. B. Phillips, *The New Testament in Modern English* (New York, NY: HarperCollins, 1962).
4. Egerton, *Flame of God*, 27.
5. Robert E. Coleman, ed., *One Divine Moment: The Asbury Revival* (Old Tappan, NJ: Fleming H. Revell, 1970), 5.
6. Jonathan Goforth, *By My Spirit* (Nappanee, IN: Evangel Publishing House), 131.
7. Frank Bartleman, *Azusa Street: An Eyewitness Account* (Alachua, FL: Bridge-Logos, 1980), 10.
8. Ibid., 49.
9. Martyn Lloyd-Jones, *Joy Unspeakable: Power and Renewal in the Holy Spirit* (Wheaton, IL: Harold Shaw Publishers, 1994), 61.
10. Glenn Bauscher, *The Original Aramaic New Testament in Plain English* (Lulu Publishing, 2010), 297.
11. Clare George Weakley Jr., ed., *The Nature of Revival* (Minneapolis, MN: Bethany House Publishing, 1987), 82–84.

Chapter Four: Revival Experience

1. Stephen Olford, *Heart Cry for Revival* (Fern, Scotland, UK: Christian Focus Publications, 2005), 146–47.
2. Henry Fish, *Handbook of Revivals: For the Use of Winners of Souls* (Boston, MA: James H. Earle, 1874), 126.
3. J. A. Wood, *Perfect Love* (Noblesville, PA: Newby Book Room, 1967), 157.
4. Fish, *Handbook of Revivals*, 130.
5. Jonathan Edwards, *Jonathan Edwards: On Revival* (Carlisle, PA: The Banner of Truth Trust, 1995), 92.
6. Mathew Backholer, *Revival Answers, True and False Revival, Genuine or Counterfeit* (United Kingdom: ByFaith Media, 2013), 125.
7. Wood, *Perfect Love*, 321–23.
8. Steve Beard, *Thunderstruck: John Wesley and the Toronto Blessing* (Wilmore, KY: Thunderstruck Communications, 1996), 5.
9. Ibid., 17–18.

10. G. E. H. Palmer, Philip Sherrard, and Kallistos Ware, eds., *The Philokalia, Volume III* (London, UK: Faber and Faber, 1986), 365.

11. Martyn Lloyd-Jones, *Joy Unspeakable: Power and Renewal in the Holy Spirit* (Wheaton, IL: Harold Shaw Publishers, 1994), 112–13.

Chapter Five: Revival Glory

1. Humphrey Wallis, *The Happy Warrior: The Story of Commissioner Elijah Cadman* (London, England, UK: Salvationist Publishing and Supplies, 1928), 107–12.

2. Gerhard Kittel, *Theological Dictionary of the New Testament, Volume II* (Grand Rapids, MI: Eerdmans, 1968), 238.

3. Gilbert Egerton, *Flame of God: Distinctives of Revival* (Belfast, Northern Ireland: Ambassador Productions, 1987), 57.

4. Tommy Welchel, *True Stories of the Miracles of Azusa Street and Beyond* (Shippensburg, PA: Destiny Image, 2013), 72.

5. S. B. Shaw, *The Great Revival in Wales* (Pensacola, FL: Christian Books, 2002), 140.

6. Egerton, *Flame of God*, 104.

7. "America's Great Revivals: The Story of Spiritual Revival in the United States, 1734–1899" *Sunday Magazine, Inc.*, 41.

8. Geoff Waugh, *Flashpoints of Revival: History's Mighty Revivals* (North Charleston, SC: BookSurge Publishing, 2009), 21.

9. Charles G. Finney, *Lectures on Revivals of Religion* (Westwood, NJ: Fleming H. Revell Co.), 124.

10. J. I. Packer, *A Quest for Godliness: The Puritan Vision of the Christian Life* (Wheaton, IL: Crossway Books, 1990), 323.

11. Frank Bartleman, *Azusa Street: An Eyewitness Account* (Alachua, FL: Bridge Logos, 1980), 68.

12. James Burns, *Revival: Their Laws and Leaders* (Grand Rapids, MI: Baker, 1960), 39.

13. Bramwell Booth, *Echoes and Memories* (London, England, UK: Hodder and Stoughton, 1925), 30–31.

Chapter Six: Revival Love

1. Jonathan Edwards, *Jonathan Edwards: On Revival* (Carlisle, PA: The Banner of Truth Trust, 1995), 149–53.
2. Geoff Waugh, *Flashpoints of Revival: History's Mighty Revivals* (North Charleston, SC: BookSurge Publishing, 2009), 149.
3. J. I. Packer, *A Quest for Godliness: The Puritan Vision of the Christian Life* (Wheaton, IL: Crossway, 1990), 323.
4. J. A. Wood, *Perfect Love* (Noblesville, PA: J. Edwin Newby, 1967), 163.
5. Ibid., 161.
6. Ibid., 168.
7. Ibid., 163–64.
8. Martyn Lloyd-Jones, *Joy Unspeakable: Power and Renewal in the Holy Spirit* (Wheaton, IL: Harold Shaw Publishers, 1994), 69–70.
9. http://www.samstorms.com/all-articles/post/the-stretching-of-sarah-edwards.
10. Ibid.
11. Waugh, *Flashpoints of Revival*, 117.
12. Ibid., 131.
13. Jean Lafrance, *My Vocation Is Love: Therese of Lisieux* (Homebush, Australia. St. Pauls, 1994), 55.
14. Ibid., 167.

Chapter Seven: Revival Humility

1. Frank Bartleman, *Azusa Street: An Eyewitness Account* (Alachua, FL: Bridge-Logos, 1980), 65–67.
2. S. B. Shaw, *The Great Revival in Wales* (Pensacola, FL: Christian Life Books, 2002), 45.
3. C. G. Bevington, *Remarkable Miracles* (Alachua, FL: Bridge-Logos, 1992), 157.
4. Marie Monsen, *The Awakening: Revival in China: 1927–1937* (Shoals, IN: Kingsley Press, 2011), 21–22.
5. S. B. Shaw, *The Great Revival in Wales*, 117.
6. Monsen, *The Awakening*, 92.
7. Bartleman, *Azusa Street*, 65.
8. Eddie Hyatt, ed., *Fire on the Earth: Eyewitness Reports from the Azusa Street Revival* (Lake Mary, FL: Creation House, 2006), 69.

Chapter Eight: Revival Witness

1. C. G. Bevington, *Remarkable Miracles* (Alachua, FL: Bridge-Logos, 1992), 139–40.
2. http://wesley.nnu.edu/wesleyctr/books/0401-0500/HDM0496.pdf.
3. John Greenfield, *Power from on High* (Bethlehem, PA: Moravian Church of America, 1928), 24.
4. N. Burwash, *Wesley's 52 Standard Sermons* (Salem, OH: Schmul Publishers, 1988), 101.
5. J. A. Wood, *Perfect Love* (Noblesville, PA: Newby Book Room, 1967), 214.
6. Eddie Hyatt, ed., *Fire on the Earth: Eyewitness Reports from the Azusa Street Revival* (Lake Mary, FL: Creation House, 2006), 44.
7. Gilbert Egerton, *Flames of God: Distinctives of Revival* (Belfast, Northern Ireland: Ambassador Production, 1987), 73.
8. Mathew Backholer, *Revival Fires and Awakenings: Thirty-Six Visitations of the Holy Spirit: A Call to Holiness, Prayer and Intercession for the Nations* (United Kingdom: ByFaith Media, 2012), 163.
9. Ibid.
10. Hyatt, *Fire on the Earth*, 12.

Chapter Nine: Revival Freedom

1. http://www.christianitytoday.com/ch/2004/issue83/eyewitness.html.
2. Duncan Campbell, *The Price and Power of Revival* (Fort Washington, PA: Christian Literature Crusade, 1962), 61.
3. J. A. Wood, *Perfect Love* (Noblesville, PA: Newby Book Room, 1967), 272.
4. Ibid., 277.
5. Jonathan Goforth, *By My Spirit* (Nappanee, IN: Evangel Publishing House), 42.
6. Campbell, *The Price and Power of Revival*, 55.
7. Wood, *Perfect Love*, 87.
8. Martyn Lloyd-Jones, *Joy Unspeakable: Power and Renewal in the Holy Spirit* (Wheaton IL: Harold Shaw Publishers, 1984), 106.
9. Wood, *Perfect Love*, 168–69.
10. Ibid., 164.

11. Geoff Waugh, *Flashpoints of Revival: History's Mighty Revivals* (North Charleston, SC: BookSurge Publishing, 2009), 78.

12. Wood, *Perfect Love*, 213.

13. Frank Bartleman, *Azusa Street: An Eyewitness Account* (Alachua, FL: Bridge-Logos, 1980), 38.

14. Clare George Weakley Jr., ed., *The Nature of Revival* (Minneapolis, MN: Bethany House Publishing, 1987), 80.

Chapter Ten: Revival Hope

1. Winkie Pratney, *Revival: Principles to Change the Word* (Springdale, PA: Whitaker House, 1984), 125–26.

2. David Bryant, *The Hope at Hand: National and World Revival for the Twenty-First Century* (Grand Rapids, MI: Baker Books, 1996), 48.

3. John Greenfield, *Power from on High* (Bethlehem: PA: The Moravian Church, 1928), 11.

4. Steve Seamands in *When God Comes* (Wilmore, KY: The Francis Asbury Society and Worldview Media, 1995).

5. Arthur Wallis, *In the Day of Thy Power: The Scriptural Principles of Revival* (London, UK: Christian Literature Crusade, 1956), 80.

6. Gilbert Egerton, *Flame of God: Distinctives of Revival* (Belfast, Northern Ireland: Ambassador Productions, 1987), 60.

7. J. B. Phillips, *The New Testament in Modern English* (New York, NY: HarperCollins, 1962).

8. J. A. Wood, *Perfect Love* (Noblesville, PA: Newby Book Room, 1967), 168.

9. Ibid., 166.

10. Mathew Backholer, *Revival Fires and Awakenings: Thirty-Six Visitations of the Holy Spirit: A Call to Holiness, Prayer and Intercession for the Nations* (United Kingdom: ByFaith Media, 2009), 30.

11. Emyr Roberts and R. G. Gruffydd, *Revival and Its Fruit* (Evangelical Library of Wales, 1987), 26–27.

12. Ibid., 35.

13. Arthur Wallis, *In the Day of Thy Power*, 65.

14. Peter Cartwright, *Autobiography of Peter Cartwright* (Nashville, TN: Abingdon Press, 1956), 144.

Chapter Eleven: Revival Worldview

1. Mathew Backholer, *Revival Fires and Awakenings: Thirty-Six Visitations of the Holy Spirit: A Call to Holiness, Prayer and Intercession for the Nations* (United Kingdom: ByFaith Media, 2012), 52–53.
2. Arthur Wallis, *In the Day of Thy Power* (London, UK: Christian Literature Crusade, 1990), 34.
3. David Bryant, *The Hope at Hand: National and World Revival for the Twenty-First Century* (Grand Rapids, MI: Baker Books, 1996), 148.
4. Ibid., 251.
5. J. I. Packer, *A Quest for Godliness: The Puritan Vision of the Christian Life* (Wheaton, IL: Crossway, 1990), 323.
6. Backholer, *Revival Fires and Awakenings*, 102.
7. Charles G. Finney, *Lectures on Revivals of Religion* (Westwood, NJ: Fleming H. Revell Co.), 318.
8. http://daibach-welldigger.blogspot.com/2012/10 /evan-roberts-hours-in-presence-of-god.html.
9. Frank Bartleman, *Azusa Street: An Eyewitness Account* (Alachua, FL: Bridge-Logos, 1980), 47.

Chapter Twelve: What's Ahead?

1. E. M. Bounds, *Power Through Prayer* (Grand Rapids, MI: Zondervan Publishing House, 1965), 87.
2. Charles G. Finney, *Lectures on Revivals of Religion* (Westwood, NJ: Fleming H. Revell Co.), 34.